Highly Respectable Families

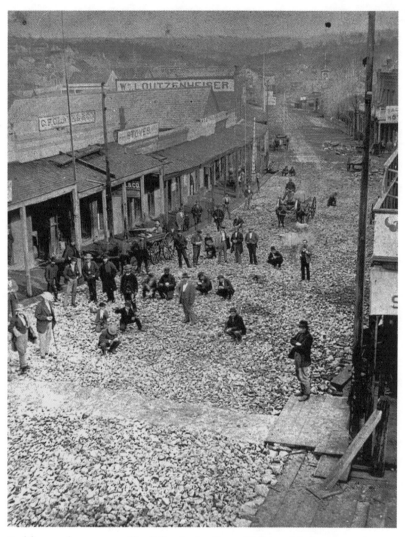

Gold-paved streets really did exist in Grass Valley; this famous 1874 photograph caught men and boys in the act of selecting precious specimens from the mine tailings newly spread along Main Street to pave that muddy thoroughfare.

Highly Respectable Families

The Cornish of Grass Valley, California 1854–1954

Shirley Ewart
with Harold T. George

Comstock Bonanza Press

GRASS VALLEY, CALIFORNIA

NEVADA COUNTY PIONEERS SERIES

PUBLISHED BY COMSTOCK BONANZA PRESS
18919 WILLIAM QUIRK DRIVE, GRASS VALLEY, CA 95945
TELEPHONE 530-273-6220

LIBRARY OF CONGRESS CATALOGING -IN-PUBLICATION DATA
EWART, SHIRLEY
HIGHLY RESPECTABLE FAMILIES : THE CORNISH OF GRASS VALLEY,
CALIFORNIA 1854-1954 / SHIRLEY EWART WITH HAROLD T. GEORGE.
P. CM. — (NEVADA COUNTY PIONEERS SERIES)
INCLUDES BIBLIOGRAPHICAL REFERENCES AND INDEX.
ISBN 0-933994-18-4 (ALK. PAPER).
1. CORNISH—CALIFORNIA—GRASS VALLEY—HISTORY.
2. BRITISH AMERICANS—CALIFORNIA—GRASS VALLEY—HISTORY.
3. CORNISH—CALIFORNIA—GRASS VALLEY—SOCIAL LIFE AND CUSTOMS.
4. BRITISH AMERICANS—CALIFORNIA—GRASS VALLEY—SOCIAL LIFE AND
CUSTOMS.
5. MINERS—CALIFORNIA—GRASS VALLEY—HISTORY.
6. CORNWALL—EMIGRATION AND IMMIGRATION—HISTORY.
7. GRASS VALLEY (CALIF.)—EMIGRATION AND IMMIGRATION—HISTORY.
8. GRASS VALLEY (CALIF.)—BIOGRAPHY.
I. GEORGE, HAROLD T., 1920– . II. TITLE. III. SERIES.
F869.G76E944 1998
979.4'37—DC21   98-21831
                                                          CIP

Contents

List of Illustrations

Hard-rock miners on "skips" prepare to descend into a Grass Valley gold-quartz mine at the rate of about 800 feet/minute.

Acknowledgments

When I first came to Grass Valley in 1979, I intended to interview people from Cornish mining families in order to understand what motivated them or their forebears to immigrate to California, how that emigration was accomplished, and what forces served to integrate the migrant into the new community. I also wanted to look at Cornish values to see if they supported or impeded acculturation to life in the U.S. Did these values change over time, and if so, how and why. How, if at all, did the process of acculturation differ for men and women? All this was worthy and academic and I set out with high hopes and a big yellow notepad.

What I had not counted on was the tremendous kindness with which these often elderly folks treated me as I asked them to tell me about their lives and those of their parents and grandparents. They shared diaries, journals, photos and press cuttings. They treated me to Cornish cream teas, pasty dinners, miner's lunch bucket cookies and "heavy cake." They introduced me to family members. It is amazing that, of all those I asked for an interview, not one turned me down. To them I owe my degree, my subsequent career, and finally, this book.

My interest in both the Cornish and the problems of migration are deep and personal. I was born in Wuhan, China, but came to England at an early age and spent much of my childhood in St. Ives, Cornwall, where my grandmother managed a small hotel. I went to school in London, but my military service in World War II brought me back again to Cornwall, and since then I have returned many times. And I, too, am an emigrant. Like every emigrant, I experienced the mixed emotions of excitement and anxiety as I packed my baggage and said goodbye to my friends and family before making the lonely journey to America to join my American-born husband. I remember the challenges of adaptation and the miseries of homesickness. I took many years to become part of the world of which my children and grandchildren are so much a part. That, too, is the experience of all who emigrate past adolescence.

My research began with a visit to the Grass Valley Methodist Church, where the minister, the Rev. Earl L. Langguth, introduced me to Harold T. George. To my delight Harold shared with me several family journals and talked eloquently about the life of his father, Harold Jewell George. Harold's sister, Carol Guinn, and her daughters, Cathy and Cindy, provided insight into the women of the George family, and through Harold I met his cousin, Lucille Simons, who was able to share her own memories of her Cornish-born father, William T. George.

I also interviewed Mary Kent, who had come to America in 1908, and Loretta Henwood Trathen, whose father and grandparents were Cornish-born. Minnie Chinn Farley, a member of the second generation, provided a fascinating picture of life in Grass Valley before World War I; her husband, Ed Farley, who had emigrated in 1929, talked about both Cornwall and Grass Valley in the 1920s and 1930s. To get an insight into how Cornish values, especially religious values, meshed with the other people living in Grass Valley, I also interviewed Salvation Army Brigadiers Howard and Eloise Sloan.

I used parts of these interviews, as well as sections from diaries and from the newspapers of the time, to illustrate my thesis, which was picked up for publication by AMS Press. Then, setting the Cornish materials aside, I went on to a career as an anthropologist, first working with Native Americans and then teaching.

It was over ten years later that my thoughts turned again to those Grass Valley interviews. I realized that so many of the people I had interviewed in 1979 had passed on. I was getting old. So, too, were the last of the people who remembered the mines. The story needed to be told for the grandchildren and for all those who loved Grass Valley and the history of this beautiful part of California. I mooted the idea for a book, and Dave Comstock of Comstock Bonanza Press was enthusiastic. But, I would need more material. Again, Harold George came to the rescue, introducing me to Cecil and Ralph Tremewan and Sibley Bennallack Hanson. Through the kindness of his great-granddaughter, Josephine Nattkemper, I was fortunate to have copies of John Coad's letters. And through Gage McKinney, of the California Cornish Cousins, I was able to meet Winnifred Rowe Cannon. This book was born!

My thanks go to all the above-mentioned, without whom this book could not have been written. I also must thank Chris Mulkey, whose maps add so much to this book. Finally, and not least, Dave Comstock who believed in this book and was both patient and flexible, when I sometimes was not, and who deserves tremendous praise for designing and publishing a book we both can be proud of.

Shirley Ewart
Tigard, Oregon

MAP AND ILLUSTRATION CREDITS:

Cover—Searls Historical Library. Frontis—Heritage Graphics (Jim Johnson). x–Juanita Browne collection. xiv—From *Nevada County Narrow Gauge* by Gerald M. Best (drawn by James Trout). xvi—By permission of the Royal Cornwall Museum (photo by J. C. Burrow). 5, 6—By permission of the Royal Cornwall Museum. 8, 9, 19, 26—Chris Mulkey. 29—From *History of Nevada County, California*, Thompson & West, 1880. 31—From *Grass Valley and Vicinity*, by J. E. Poingdestre, 1895; Searls Historical Library. 34—From *Grass Valley and Vicinity*, by J. E. Poingdestre, 1895. 42—Courtesy of George Perrin. 46—Juanita Brown collection. 48—From *Grass Valley and Vicinity*, by J. E. Poingdestre, 1895. 49—Harold T. George. 51—Courtesy of George Perrin. 53—Courtesy of the Grass Valley Methodist Church. 55—Courtesy of George Perrin. 56—Grass Valley Video History Museum (gift of John E. Nettell, photo by Edgar A. Pickering). 59—Juanita Browne collection (Tyler Photo); Searls Historical Library. 64—By permission of the Royal Cornwall Museum (photo by S. Dalby-Smith). 67—Courtesy of Sibley Bennallack Hansen. 73—Courtesy of Sibley Bennallack Hansen; *Grass Valley and Vicinity*, by J. E. Poingdestre, 1895. 75, 80, 84—Juanita Browne collection. 85—Courtesy of Harriet Jakobs (Alfred M. Kramm collection). 89—Courtesy of Winnifred Rowe Cannon. 97—Juanita Browne collection. 99—Courtesy of Winnifred Rowe Cannon. 101, 103—Juanita Browne collection. 106—Searls Historical Library (gift of Nancy I. Burdett). 109—Courtesy of Cecil Tremewan. 115—Searls Historical Library; Grass Valley Video History Museum. 123—From *Grass Valley and Vicinity*, by J. E. Poingdestre, 1895. 128—By permission of the Royal Cornwall Museum. 130—Grass Valley Video History Museum. 131—Courtesy of Sibley Bennallack Hansen. 137—Comstock Bonanza collection. 161—Courtesy of Sibley Bennallack Hansen (photo by Don Weller).

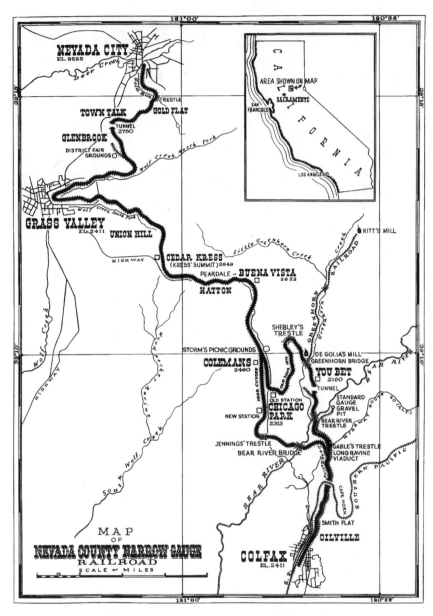

Route of the Nevada County Narrow Gauge Railroad. The original 1876 bridge crossing over Bear River carried travelers to Grass Valley by way of Shebley's Trestle and Pond. The later 1908 route bypassed the old You Bet station and rejoined theoriginal line at Storms' Picnic Grounds, where the annual United Sunday School outings took place for many years.

Introduction
The Cornish and Their Story

T he movements of tribes and of peoples is a phenomenon as old as human history. Since long before the time when Abraham left the land of Haran, people have sought greener pastures. Some were pushed out of their native fields by natural disasters of flood or famine, or by the influx of marauding armies; some were pulled by tales of land flowing with milk and honey, or streets paved with gold. Among the latter were the Cornish mining families who left their beautiful land with its rocky shores and misty moors and traveled to the gold fields of Grass Valley, California, to seek their fortunes.

Focusing on seven families during the time frame 1854– 1954, this book uses diaries, newspaper reports and oral histories to tell the story of these Cornish emigrants. We learn what motivated the men and women to leave Cornwall. We share with them the hardships of the steamship journey to the New World; and we observe how they became acculturated to life in America.

Diaries and memories remind us that these were a very social people. They thoroughly enjoyed their church teas, bazaars and Sunday School picnics, loved parades and exercized considerable musical talent in the several choirs and bands that were a feature of life both in Cornwall and in Grass Valley.

However, the most important legacies they handed on to their children were Cornish values of hard work, pride in themselves and their families and a sense of community, as well as religious commitment involving strong belief in the Biblical virtues. In 1853 a newspaper characterized the residents of Grass Valley as "highly respectable families." This is exactly the way the Cornish themselves would have hoped to be remembered.

The Carn Brae mine on the hill looms over the town of Redruth, Cornwall, in this photograph taken from Church Lane in the 1890s

Chapter 1
Cornwall—The Homeland

"Cornwall is a pore and very barren country of al maner
thing, except Tyn and Fysshe."
—Andrew Borde 1542

The County of Cornwall is that slender toe of England which pushes out into the Atlantic. Never more than 80 miles long, this sea-girt land is separated from the rest of England by the River Tamar, which so bisects the peninsula that only a slim four miles prevents the county from becoming an island.

The climate of the land is mild and damp, tempered by the warmth of the Atlantic Current in the winter and the south-westerly winds year round. Rainfall is heavy, but snow and ice are rather rare. Writers have described the bare hills and wild shores of this tip of England, but away from the coast and in the river valleys there are pleasant green fields with grazing cows, source of the rich cream for which Cornwall is famous. The truck farms of the "Cornish Riviera" provide early fruit and vegetables for the London markets, as well as the daffodils that bring a hint of spring to shivering London and snowbound Edinburgh.

Earlier inhabitants of this remote outpost of Europe had been replaced by successive waves of Celtic peoples long before the Roman invasion of the first century A.D. We know of a tribe of *Cornovii* who lived in the Severn Valley, and it is possible that the Romans encouraged the migration of the tribe to fill the sparsely populated southwest peninsula. It is also possible that the Romans simply used the term "Cornovii" to apply to the group of people who lived in the *cornu*, meaning horn or peninsula.

Brythonic Celtic, ancestor of both Welsh and Cornish, was spoken throughout England and Wales and much of Scotland when the Romans arrived. For many generations thereafter, Latin served as a lingua franca and was the language of government, of trade, of culture and education, and above all the language of writing, so that over the centuries hundreds of Latin words were borrowed into the Celtic language as it was spoken in Cornwall; e.g. Cornish "fenester" from Latin *fenestra* (window), and Cornish "mor" from Latin *mare* (sea).

Long after English had become the language of the rest of Britain, the inhabitants of the peninsula retained their own Cornish language, and through the 16th century few spoke any other tongue. In the 17th century, the insistence that the English Book of Common Prayer be used in Cornish churches caused riots; the Cornish refused to worship in a tongue which was more alien to them even than the traditional Latin. The Cornish language finally died out by the end of the 18th century, but remains in place names and personal names, and in some mining terms.[1]

From the earliest times these Celtic peoples had mined tin, and had exported both tin and copper at least as early as 500 B.C., finding their ore in surface deposits which resulted from the breakdown and weathering of the lodes. These "Old Men," as the early miners are called by the Cornish, were competent geologists who understood the characteristics of the various lodes and knew the best way to exploit them. Most were "tin streamers" who dug out the deposits and then used large wooden bowls to "pan" them in a stream, allowing the heavy ore to settle and the rest of the material to be raked off. A later improvement in technique involved the diversion of the stream to the site of the deposits.

The tin streamers worked in family groups as independent operators. In accordance with the "Charter for the Stannaries" (from Latin *stannum* for tin) granted by Richard I (1157–1199) the tinners were free of most taxes and of most military service and obeyed only those rules laid down in the Charter. Until 1752 a "Stannary Court" dealt with disputes over mining rights and tenures. Because through the years every square yard of the mining district was plotted into "setts" that could be reckoned as chattels and sold or bequeathed, there was much litigation as to ownership of the mineral rights.

Streaming remained the principal method of mining before the 16th century. By the 17th century the ever deeper tin workings revealed the lodes of copper ore; until the mid-18th century tin and copper were worked together, although tin remained the more important Cornish export. Between 1740 and 1755 the number of mines producing copper had almost trebled, however the total value of copper exports did not exceed the value of tin exports until about 1782.[2]

The problems of mining the deeper lode ores were considerable and required new and ingenious inventions. Reaching the "stope" or working surface of the lode involved tunnelling through the hard rock, and then splitting that rock in order to win the ore. When working at the new depths, it was necessary to get rid of the water that seeped in both from the water table and, as the mines probed under the sea floor, from the sea itself. Finally, there were the problems of hoisting out the ore and of extracting the valuable mineral content.

Early miners had used shovels made of wood, or of metal-tipped wood, to break ground. To split the rock they used either metal wedges, or fire, or quick lime. By the 17th century gunpowder was introduced for splitting rock and gunpowder factories were built in the county. Before the safety fuse was invented in 1831, the gunpowder was placed in shotholes drilled in the rock, and then ignited with a fuse of quills or straws; a very dangerous procedure. In the 1860s Albert Nobel developed compositions enabling the safe use of nitroglycerine, and this eventually replaced gunpowder for blasting.

Flooding in the mines was always a problem. Well before the 16th century, "adits" or small tunnels were dug through the hillside to drain off the water at the lowest point of the workings, but if the floor of the stope was flat, it was necessary either to bail out the water, or to use a pump, which was at first a simple contraption of buckets or rags on an endless chain. In the 18th century the invention of the steam engine allowed the mechanization, not only of the water pump, but also of the hoist by which the ore was brought to the surface. Before the 19th century, the miners used a length of hemp rope attached to a simple round "kibble" or basket. In 1820 the hemp was re-placed by chains, and after 1850 by steel rope.

The Cornish mine dominated the neighborhood and em-ployed not only miners, but carpenters, sawyers, smiths, engine men, coal meters (who bought coal at the coal yard) and raisers and "whim men," who brought the ore to the surface. Above ground ("to grass") were men, women and children who "dressed" the ore. It was usual for children to start work at the surface at the age of eight or nine, although many were younger. A Commission to inquire into all non-coal mines of Great Britain made its report in the *Parliamentary Papers of 1842*. Captain Charles Thomas of Dolcoath testified:

> Sometimes a father or mother will come and say, "I have this little child, and I do not know what to do with it; I can scarcely get bread for it; will you take it?" and sometimes we yield to that and take the child in to such work as it can do, but it is very light work.

The younger girls picked pieces of ore, the younger boys washed ore. The hardest work done by the boys was "jigging," sieving copper ore in water. This necessitated standing doubled up in the water, and it is reported that some boys coughed up blood. In 1842 the youngest boy underground was only eight years old, but later laws prohibited lads under ten from work-ing underground.

The youngest children would receive two or three pennies a day, and it is said the money was carried home to parents. These children worked ten hours a day in summer, an hour less in winter, with an hour or half an hour for lunch. Overtime was not uncommon, and in addition most families had to walk for an hour or more to reach their cottages, often in cold and wet weather.

By age nine the children could make their own contracts, and by this age, boys might be set to work the air machines or fans that forced air from the entrance to the unventilated shaft ends, and they also wheeled barrows. James Hosking remembered being given charge of the two horses that worked in the whim which raised and lowered the kibbles or baskets that hauled ore

Cornish boy miners "tramming" at the 406 fathom level of Cook's Kitchen Mine about 1893.

to the surface.[4] The *British Parliamentary Papers* reported that boys generally worked with their fathers or near relatives who were considerate of the youngsters and who taught them the skills they needed. By about age 12, boys' and girls' jobs differed: the boys began to wheel the heavy barrows of ore, and the girls became "bal maidens." Along with older women they spalled (broke up) the larger rocks with long handled hammers, and then "bucked" the resulting smaller pieces on an anvil. This last was extremely hard work, as the women worked while seated in cramped positions in cold, often wet sheds. In 1842 a woman might earn a shilling a day, but eight or nine pence was average.

It is estimated that in 1827 there were 2,276 women working in the copper and tin mines of Cornwall. As the industry expanded the numbers grew to 5,764. During the 1850s many mines began to shift their production from copper to tin, which required fewer women, and when the price of copper fell sharply during the 1850s, both men and women lost their jobs. In 1871 there were still 4,450 women employed at mine work in Cornwall, but the introduction of new machinery brought a virtual end of work for bal maidens.[5] Mary Kent, however, had clear memories of women employed at Carn Brea Mine as late as 1913 (see Chapter 10).

The new technology needed to reach deeper lodes increased the amount of capital needed far beyond the resources of the individual mine owner. "Cost book" companies were formed into which 64 or 128 shareholders paid money to finance the mining operations, and from which each drew profits according to the prosperity of the venture. These shareholders might be representatives of copper-smelting interests from Bristol or from South Wales, or they might be "London Adventurers." However, many local families found it very profitable to form their own companies. As more mines were worked by the cost-book system, actual operations demanded supervision by technologists, and a class of "mine captains" filled the need for skilled direction of the increasing numbers of workers both below and above the ground. The company employed miners under one of two forms of contract: "Tutworkers" or task

"Bal maidens" interrupt their work of breaking ore with hammers long enough to have a picture taken at Tincroft in the 1890s.

workers provided their own tools, candles and dynamite and were paid a set amount per unit of work done, e.g. per fathom advanced, square fathom of lode stoped or tunnelled, or weight of deposit mined; "Tributers" were "pares" or teams of men who functioned as independent contractors. Tributer groups bid against each other for the pitch they would work, and were then paid a proportion of the value of the ore won.[6]

Until well into the 20th century, the economy of Cornwall depended almost entirely on the price of copper and tin. As prices rose and fell, so did the standard of living of the population. In 1787 great copper deposits were found in Anglesea, off the coast of Wales. As copper from this abundant new source flooded the market, prices fell and many Cornish mines closed, including Dolcoath, the greatest then in operation. Nevertheless, by 1801 there were 75 mines in Cornwall employing 16,000 people, and in 1838 there were 200 mines with 30,000 people employed. By this time there were 170 steam-powered pumping engines and 120 steam-powered stamping machines. The profits were huge. North Roskear mine at Camborne, which had opened at the end of the 18th century, reported that from June 1834 to June 1842 ore worth £213,320 ($1,066,660) had been produced at a profit of £490,000 ($1,026,069). At about the same time (1827) it was recorded that the average wage of a tributer was £2 18s 2d a month ($14.51), while a tutworker paid by the fathom might expect to make £2 13s 8d ($13.31).[7]

Fortunately, mining was by no means the sole occupation of these people, at least until the mid-19th century. Cornish mines did not house their workers, and most mining families lived in the country on a small patch of land on which potatoes or other crops could be raised. The miner would usually lease the house and an acre of so surrounding it, or even more frequently, lease the ground and build his own house. He and his heirs paid a nominal rent during the term of the lease, which was normally for the duration of three lives named in the lease. The practice was to name three children over four or five years old and the

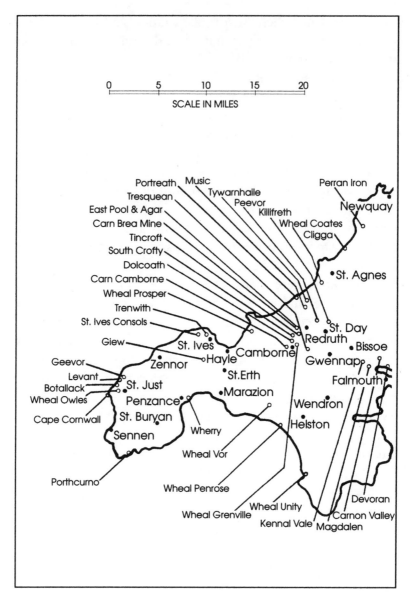

Map 1. Mining areas in Western Cornwall.

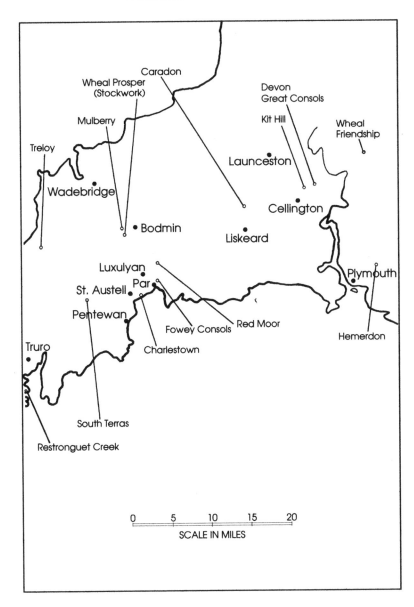

Map 2. Mining areas in Eastern Cornwall.

lease would remain valid until all those names as "lives" had died.[8]

Commonly a cow would also be rented, the family receiving milk and undertaking to rear the calf and return it at the end of the year, while the farmer provided winter feed and bore the loss if the animal died.[9] Some miners also kept pigs, but generally not much meat was eaten. However, because the mining family did have easy access to the sea, fish provided much of the necessary protein in the otherwise largely vegetarian diet. Thus agriculture and fishing supplemented mining, and only when all three failed did the people go hungry.

In the 1840s, however, a combination of events reduced many of the once independent mining families to destitution. The first threat to the economy was the potato blight, which affected the crop that was the mainstay of the countryman's diet. Without potatoes it was necessary to purchase grain, and speculators had kept wheat and barley prices exorbitantly high throughout the decade. At the same time, the first half of the 19th century marked a period of great population growth in Cornwall as in the rest of England. A. K. Hamilton Jenkin notes the increases from 1801 to 1861 as follows:[10]

1801-11	1811-21	1821-31	1831-41	1841-51	1851-61
plus 14%	plus 18%	plus 16%	plus 13%	plus 3%	plus 3%

With more children to feed, and less food to do it on, the working people came close to starvation. Hamilton Jenkin quotes T. Oliver of Gulval's *Autobiography of a Cornish Miner*. Oliver remembers a diet of barley gruel, barley pasty, barley cake and stewed potatoes and turnips with a little fat; hardly enough to nourish a working man or woman, let alone a growing child or a nursing mother. At that time (1840) Oliver's father earned £2 5s a month, the standard wage for surface work. Oliver himself earned 10s a month. The combined salary of £2 15s provided for five people.[11] It is no wonder these years were known "the hungry forties."

At about the same time, because of increasingly efficient mining methods and the greedy demands of the owners for higher and higher profits, the copper lodes were being exhausted, and many of the less economic mines had to close. This might well mean starvation for whole families. Seeking a better life, a few miners sold their belongings, borrowed from friends and relatives and left for North or South America, South Africa or Australia.

In the mines still being worked, dwindling productivity forced the working of deeper and deeper levels, and conditions in the mines became increasingly hazardous to the miner's health. It was not unusual for men to work at depths of nearly 2,000 feet, and until the 1840s, when machinery was introduced, these levels had to be reached by climbing down ladders; heart problems from the prolonged overexertion were common. In addition to temperatures that reached 80 or 90 degrees F, the men had to contend with dripping dampness, and since there were no facilities for drying out their clothes, they were forced to walk home cold and wet, which often led to pneumonia. Also, many of the deep levels lay under the sea and the constant exposure to the seepage of salt water caused boils and skin lesions. Lack of ventilation and new methods of blasting that increased harmful dust led to "miner's consumption" (sometimes called "rocks on the chest" or "miner's psthisis), and this was the most usual non-accidental cause of death. The average Cornish miner did not live to see his 41st birthday; those who were not killed by accidents perished of exhaustion and excessive toil.

In spite of the severity of their conditions, the Cornish did not react by uniting in political action. Although there were bread riots in the 1840s, by and large the miners accepted their lot with stoic fortitude. For one thing, the Cornish were individualists who had rarely been successful at uniting for any purpose. Not only were villages scattered, but there was traditional friction or even animosity between people from different villages. In addition, the system of labor had contended teams of men against each other, rather than against the owners, and this precluded worker solidarity.

Another factor that made it difficult for the miners to take an adversary position against owners was the structure of Cornish society. Through the years all classes had become interrelated, and within the same family there might be adventurers, merchants, captains and miners. There were also deep-rooted feelings of respect between the miners and the large land-owning families.

Finally, and not the least important, the teachings of John Wesley had received the wholehearted endorsement of the Cornish. Wesley had emphasized that life was brief and hard, merely a preparation for the world to come. The exhortation, "Look not to the things of this world," appeared to restrain any attempts to change the status quo.

Cornwall led the world in the production of copper and tin during the 1850s. In 1857 copper production hit a record 209,000 tons. It was noted, however that there had been a drop in the metallic content of the ores mined, and in *The West Briton* of February 25, 1859, it was reported that shareholders of Fowey Consuls were warned: "Many of our old pitches are wearing out."[12]

This was a period of high employment in Cornwall, and the wage of an adult male reached £2 8s a month, an amount criticized by some as "giving greater opportunity of indulging in sensual appetites."[13] Nevertheless, J. R. Leifchild (writing in 1857) describes the miners as "wan and mine beaten"[14] and he later remarks that "the fatigue of the miners is excessive, and the waste of flesh, mental energy and animal spirits is grievous."[15]

In the same year Dr. Richard Quiller Couch reported in *The West Briton* of November 27 that in the whole county of Cornwall 64.17% of all males and 45.73% of all females died before reaching five years of age. Most of these deaths occurred in the first year of life.[16] Epidemics were rife. According to *The West Briton* of August 19, 1864, in the village of Calstock more than 150 deaths had occurred that year; the total parish population was only 7,500.[17]

The overcrowding of the cottages must certainly have played a part in the spread of disease. In 1846 conditions had been bad enough to invite a "Parliamentary Inquiry," and it was reported that nine persons in a two-room cottage was not unusual. In 20 years, things had changed little.

Copper continued to be the most important export until the 1860s, but after 1863 copper production was down and at the same time the discovery of great new copper deposits at Lake Superior in the United States, together with the increased output from the Spanish mines in South America, brought a fall in the price of the metal. 1865 was disastrous. One by one the mines closed down. Those that hoped to survive resorted to desperate economies, cutting back on important maintenance, laying off men, and requiring those not laid off to work longer hours for reduced wages. But these measures were largely ineffective, and by 1867 copper mining had ceased in the western part of the county.

To make matters worse, an unusually cold winter with heavy snows was followed by rains which flooded several of the remaining mines. *The West Briton* of April 1867 reported that half the miners in Cornwall were starving. Wages for the few who were still working had been cut by a third, and those families without a wage earner were forced to seek relief in the workhouse. Three out of four miners in Cornwall had been employed in the copper mines, and though tin mining did continue and even increase slightly, it did not provide employment to the large numbers of unemployed copper miners.[18]

Emigration presented an extremely practical solution for the predicament of the miners. Higher wages in the boom years had allowed families to accumulate the minimum amount of capital needed to stake a willing kinsman who would try his fortune outside the county. Some turned to London and the Midland towns, but for most emigration meant a journey overseas.

Because men worked in family teams, it was quite common for them to emigrate together, or at least for the senior member to send for his "pare" as soon as he got established. Whole families of brothers left, one by one, for Africa, New Zealand, Australia and America. Many of these joined uncles or cousins who had managed to make the journey in the preceding three decades.

During the years 1871 to 1881, one-third of the mining population of Cornwall left the county, and the 1881 census shows an overall decrease in population of 8.9% and a 24% decrease in the population of miners.[19] A very large number of these miners came to seek their fortunes in the gold mines of Nevada County, California.

NOTES (SEE BIBLIOGRAPHY FOR FULL ATTRIBUTIONS)

1. Today there is great interest in the revival of the Cornish language. Textbooks have been published and there are classes for both adults and children, as well as an annual "Gorsedd" which features Cornish choirs, poetry, dance and drama. Stories and poems may be found on the following web sites:
   "Welcome to Cornish" http://www.bbmedia.com.au/cornish/ (Lycos)
   "Tabm Kernuack: A Bit of Modern Cornish"
   http://www.ex.ac.uk~ajbeer/aust/htm (Yahoo)
2. John Rowe, *Cornwall in the Age of the Industrial Revolution,* pp 56–58.
3. British Parliamentary Papers. *Children's Employment Commission First Report,* Vol 6.
4. Judith Cook, *Close to the Earth,* pp 28–30.
5. Gill Burke, "The Decline of the Independent Bal Maiden," pp 182–184.
6. By the 20th century these "Cost Book Companies" had become limited liability companies and the system of tutwork and tribute had disappeared.
7. J. R. Leifchild, *Cornwall and Its Mines and Miners,* p 144.
8. Rowe, *The Hardrock Men,* p 22.
9. *Ibid,* p 7.
10. Hamilton A. K. Jenkin, *The Cornish Miner,* p 172.
11. *Ibid,* p 251.
12. Rowe, *Cornwall. . . . ,* p 307.
13. Jenkin, *Cornwall and Its People,* p 34.
14. Leifchild, p 34.
15. *Ibid,* p 157.
16. Rowe, *Cornwall . . . ,* p 312.
17. R. M. Barton, *Life in Cornwall in the Late Nineteenth Century,* p 121.
18. Rowe, *Cornwall . . . ,* p 319.
19. Jenkin, *The Cornish Miner,* p 34.

Chapter 2
The Journey—From the Old World to the New

Cornish miners first reached the United States early in the eighteenth century. In 1737 Peter Grubb, son of a Cornish emigrant, acquired and named the Cornwall iron deposit in Pennsylvania.[1] In the 1820s, the Cornish were the first foreigners in the Wisconsin and Illinois lead regions, and by the 1830s the emigration had swelled to a flood. *The West Briton* of April 6, 1832, displayed a headline, "The Exodus Begins," and reported:

> The rage for emigration that now prevails in the North of this County is wholly unprecedented in Cornwall. In different parishes from 200 to 300 persons each have either departed or are preparing to leave for Canada or the United States.[2]

For the Cornish, the essential motivation for emigration was economic. Conditions in both Cornwall and the rest of England were bad all during the 1830s and into the 1840s. In 1842 over one million people in England were receiving poor relief. There was a movement at this time to use emigration as a deliberate policy to lessen the pressure caused by poverty and overpopulation, and assisted emigration was suggested. The government turned down the suggestion, stating that people were already emigrating in sufficiently large numbers.[3]

Political factors may also have contributed to the general unrest. The political movement for the repeal of the Corn Laws[4] was at its height, while from 1839 to 1848 the efforts of the Chartists to obtain suffrage for all male citizens, the secret ballot and annual Parliamentary elections had led to a general strike, riots, and in 1848, a large public demonstration. Even in Cornwall, where there was less social consciousness than in the North, ideas as to the rights of the working man were being bruited about. The political democracy of the United States may have seemed ideologically attractive.

In 1848 the discovery of gold in California gave an immediate stimulus to a fresh wave of emigrants. News of the gold rush reached Cornish mining communities, and almost exactly one year after the first discovery of gold, *The West Briton* of January 19, 1849, ran an advertisement under the headline "Cornwall Association for Streaming for Gold in California." The advertisement solicited the "sale of 4,000 shares (on the cost book system) at a deposit of 5s. a share," and went on to say:

> In a report of the United States Government it is stated that "Gold is to be found in almost every locality, on the lands, on the mountains, in valleys, in rocks and streams, in rivers, gullies and holes, in fact almost everywhere, that the extent of the gold region may safely be estimated at not less than 500 miles by 150 and is capable of employing 200,000 individuals for centuries to come." If there ever was a call for the skilled labour of Cornwall as a tin streaming, tin washing, and mining county, this gold district demands it. For prospectuses, and to secure shares, apply to Mr. Joseph Wood, Sec. pro tem., St. Austell.[5]

On August 30, 1850, *The West Briton* reported:

> A company has been formed in Breage for the purpose of sending parties to the gold diggings of California. The capital has been all subscribed, and eight men who are going out have been provided with tents and working tools. The company is to be managed upon the same principles as some of our leading mines, and a code of rules and regulations have been compiled, which appear to meet every requirement. This is the first company of the kind carried out in Cornwall.[6]

Letters from those who already had emigrated received wide circulation and even newspaper publication, and certainly must have sparked the desire to emigrate. *The West Briton* of August 29, 1851, published such a letter from John Roberts to his brother in Camborne. Roberts had written:

> Gold seems to be the object of all; talk with whomsoever I may on the motives which brought them to California, there is the same answer with one and all; that is to get a pile of

gold, and return to their families and friends in better circumstances than they were in before they left their homes.[7]

The newspapers carried advertisements by agents of the various shipping companies. These agents described the sailing ships with enthusiasm. In 1853 Bowman, Grinnell and Company advertised in *The Liverpool Mercury*:

> The ships are nearly all new, constructed with particular regard to strength and durability, and commanded by Captains of undoubted nautical skill, experience, and humanity. The good health, which has been particularly remarked always to prevail among the passengers on board them, affords a convincing proof that everything calculated to ensure the convenience and comfort of the emigrants has been strictly adhered to.[8]

Similar advertisements appeared in all contemporary newspapers. The agents for the shipping lines, who had offices in most county towns throughout England, promised to store luggage free, to transfer money to America and to sell tickets valid for interior destinations.

In addition to the advertisements, there were also circulating in England both guide books and "penny pamphlets" which extolled the charms of those states which wished to encourage immigration. Many of these were written to arouse the romantic instincts of the reader. Particular mention was made of the egalitarianism of the States where "no man had to tip his hat." In *Semi-tropical California* by Benjamin Truman, published in 1876, California was pictured as a paradise where land was cheap.[9] The Cornish, however, were less concerned with land than with the opportunity to practice their skill as hard-rock miners.

Having decided to immigrate to California, the next step was to decide on the route. Those who came before 1850 had a choice of only two alternative. There was the voyage around the Horn, which took four or five months; this did allow the passenger to proceed all the way without changing mode of transportation, and therefore was particularly useful for those traveling with a great deal of luggage, but it was not much favored by working class passengers coming from Cornwall.

There was also the option of taking a ship across the Atlantic, either to New York, or possibly to New Orleans or Galveston, and then proceeding by railway, river boat and wagon train. This too was a long and hazardous trip, with all the discomfort of hot, dry and dusty prairies, difficult river crossings and freezing mountain passes, to say nothing of dangers from still not pacified Indians.

Most of the Cornish who came to California before 1850 did come by the overland route, and most of these persons worked for some time in the Middle West before going on to California from Michigan, Wisconsin or Illinois.

An alternative route which cut the sea voyage to six weeks was inaugurated in 1850 and was recommended by the travel books as "most reasonable, comfortable and time saving." The traveler took a ship from Liverpool to New York and then from New York proceeded by ship to Aspinwall (Colón) in Panama. Then a "bungo" or canoe was boarded for the three-day journey up the Chagres River to Cruces, where mules could be hired. The final 12 miles was a rough trail ride through mountain passes to Panama City on the Pacific coast. Here the traveler boarded another ship for the voyage to San Francisco.

Many of the younger passengers simply hiked the whole 40 miles along the riverbank and over the mountains; they could either carry their own baggage or send it by mule train.[10] William Trevorrow described how his grandparents, together with their brothers, sisters, cousins and friends, left Cornwall in 1850 by sailing ship; the whole party hiked across the Isthmus along the Chagres River in order to get the boat for California.[11] By 1851 more than half of all travelers to the West Coast came across the Isthmus, and this was made even more convenient when the Panama Railway was completed in 1855 and the journey was reduced to a three-hour train ride.

The disadvantages of the Panama Route included the ever present threat of yellow fever, and the rugged and mosquito infested terrain. Another alternative was offered by the Nica-

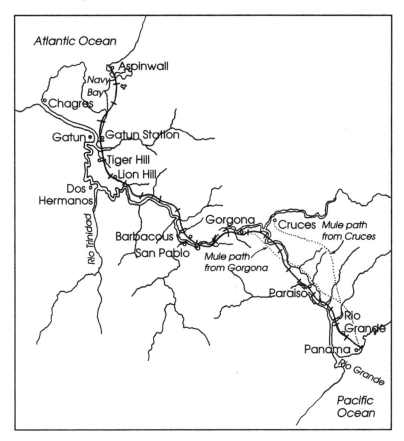

Map 3. Route of the Panama Railroad

ragua Steamship Company, which advertised in the *Grass Valley Telegraph* on April 18, 1854. The new route was publicized as "12 miles of land carriage on a macadamized road," and the company offered the use of a "land car" for this portion of the journey. The advertisement fails to note that the actual distance was 134 miles and that most of the journey had to be made by canoe!

We can be sure that all these alternative ways of travel were much debated by the prospective emigrants as they discussed the voyage with their friends, for most of the emigration journeys were not solitary experiences. Cornish miners had always worked in teams of "pares" and it was not unusual for teammates to emigrate together. Most likely, several from the same town or village would be leaving at the same time; typically groups would consist of several young men, perhaps one or two older married couples with children, and one or two younger women with small children traveling to join their husbands. Members of the group could thus help each other on the voyage and in the confusion of the arrival in the new land.

The early advertisements, which portrayed the sailing ships as safe and healthy and gave the impression they operated on regular schedules, flew in the face of the evidence. Once at sea, the emigrant was at the mercy of captain and crew as well as of the weather. Numerous wrecks occurred, due to the condition of the ships, most of which had been designed to carry lumber to the British Isles, and carried passengers on the return voyage with little more consideration than if they had been freight.

Emigrants provided their own food for the voyage, in order to supplement the meager and unpalatable rations. There was also a great deal of overcrowding, and from 1826 to 1842 there were mass epidemics of typhus and other infectious diseases.

A Passenger Act was passed in 1835 in an effort to regulate the trade and curb the more unscrupulous ship masters, but the 1845 *Report of the Colonial Land Commissioners* on prosecution of those offending the Act gives ample evidence of abuses even in the 1840s. Further Passenger Acts were passed by Parliament in 1842 and 1851.[12]

Catherine Parr Traill, writing in 1855 for prospective immigrants to Canada, quoted Vere Foster, author of the pamphlet *Advice to Migrants*. Foster, a philanthropist interested in promoting emigration, himself crossed the Atlantic in steerage so that he might "test in his own person the privation and discomforts to which the poorer emigrant passengers are exposed and be enabled to afford suitable advice respecting the voyage out to others."[13]

The fare to New York from Liverpool is quoted as £4 10s (approximately $18), and each passenger 14 years old and upwards was entitled by law to certain provisions. These included water, bread, flour, oatmeal, salt pork, sugar, tea and molasses. In 1852 the Passenger Act had required that all articles needing to be cooked must be issued in a cooked state. Foster remarks: "This excellent parliamentary regulation is often evaded." In addition, each passenger was entitled to lodgings on board from the day of sailing, and for 48 hours after arriving in America.

During the 37-day voyage from Liverpool to New York Foster consumed the additional food which he took with him, including wheaten flour, bacon, butter, "hard baked bread," tea, brown sugar, salt, and bread soda for raising cakes. He suggested that cheese, herrings, potatoes and onions be added to this list as well as preserved milk. He also listed the household ware he needed on board, including a water can, saucepan, frying pan, washbasin, teapot, kettle, tin plates and mugs, knives, forks and spoons, and soap. He added a barrel and padlock for holding provisions, a straw mattress, blankets, rugs and sheets and tells his readers they should also bring a covered slop pail and a broom.[14]

The comfort aboard the ship was minimal. The steerage passengers slept below the decks in six-foot-square berths. Men were given the upper berths and women lower; there is evidence that to have put single women in a separate compartment might have exposed them to grave danger of molestation by the crew.[15] Only in 1855 did the law require "at least two water closets, with two additional per hundred passengers," and the same year saw separate sleeping quarters prescribed for male single passengers.

The completion of the transcontinental railroad in 1869 not only cut the length of the trip to Grass Valley from a minimum of 6 weeks to a mere 18 days, but also allowed the passengers to considerably cut down on the provisions needed, since the journey was so much shorter. Nevertheless, steerage conditions remained primitive until the 20th century. Only when third class service was introduced by the White Star Line were dining rooms and some two- and four-berth cabins provided for the lowest class of passengers, and this only on British ships. Foreign ships continued to use the old "steerage" accommodations until World War I.[16]

Planning what to take and how to carry it was a major

undertaking, especially for the woman emigrant. The man, whether in the 1850s or later, could travel light. He needed, of course, the shipboard supplies, but apart from those, a few clothes, some favorite tools, perhaps a Bible and a few photographs sufficed. For the woman, faced with the responsibility of moving one or more children half way round the world, and then setting up a home for herself and her family, planning was a different matter. Catherine Traill advised the woman emigrant to bring good shoes (if possible, two pairs for each person) and also yardage of flannel, merino and tweed. Strong checked cloth for aprons would be needed, as well as "fine white cotton stockings."[17] Although the emigrant knew clothing could be purchased in the States, she probably also had heard that prices in America were high. In any case, once she arrived she might expect any available money would be used to set up her household; it behooved her to bring with her whatever clothing she and her children would need for the first year or so. Naturally, the young woman would want to make a good impression in the new community. Cornish women liked to dress well, and the money earned at the mine head or in the factory was spent carefully to outfit the family appropriately.

In addition to clothes for herself and her children, the married woman would need to bring bed linen and household and kitchen utensils, as well as tableware and china. She would also want to bring a few small knickknacks as mementos of home; perhaps some photographs or picture postcards of her home town or village. And, of course, the family photographs and her Bible would be packed. All these preparations must have taken time, and may have taken her mind off the reality of parting—perhaps forever—from her family.

When all the plans were made and the packing was done, there was nothing left to do but to say goodbye to friends and relatives and leave. From the earliest times it was the custom for the whole chapel congregation to bid Godspeed to the emigrant, and through the years the chapel must have seen many such farewell ceremonies. Ernest Brokenshire, who left St. Austell about 1910, recalled for A. L. Rowse that on Sunday at

Carclaze Methodist Church it was the regular thing to read out the names of those leaving and sing "God be with you till we meet again." Of course, the younger members probably would meet again in Michigan or Wisconsin, Arizona or California, but many an older person must have cried a little, sustained only by the firm faith that all would surely meet again in the next world.

Once on the ship, as well as during the difficult overland journey, we should note that there was somewhat of a difference between the roles of men and those of women. Women traveled as wives and mothers and were kept busy caring for their children, who were often sick on the voyage. In the early days, they were also responsible for preparing all the family's meals. They probably had little time to brood about their own homesickness or to think too much about the challenges to be faced on arrival in America. The men, on the other hand, were far more likely to be responsible only for themselves and, unlike the women, they were not "employed" in their usual occupations while on the journey. This may have meant that they had far more time both to worry about the families they had left behind and to embroider their expectations of the new country. For the men then, the journey may have been a time of some apprehension.

There was one factor, however, which did help to maintain the links between the old world and the new and so cushioned the impact of leaving home. Emigrants rarely traveled alone; parties varying from 4 to 13 members were formed in Cornwall and traveled together to the United States. Especially in the days of the long voyage via Panama, close friendships must have formed among the small groups of fellow travelers and many of these friendships would survive in the American setting.

NOTES

1. A. L. Rowse, *The Cousin Jacks*, p 96.
2. R. M. Barton, *Life in Cornwall in the Early Nineteenth Century*, p 217.
3. W. A. Carrothers, *Emigration from the British Isles*, p 181.

4. The Corn Laws, passed in 1815, excluded the importation of almost all foreign grain (wheat) until the price of domestic wheat rose to a specified high level. In 1828 the importation of grain was permitted, but a sliding scale of import duties still protected domestic wheat. After years of campaigning by the Anti-Corn Law League, in 1846 Parliament repealed the Corn Laws.

5. R. M. Barton, *Life in Cornwall in the Mid Nineteenth Century*, p 166.

6. *Ibid*, p 190.

7. Rowse, p 243.

8. Philip Taylor, *The Distant Magnet*, p 68.

9. *Ibid*, p 72.

10. John Easter Minter, *The Chagres*, p 211.

11. Norman H. Harries, *Cornish and Welsh Mining Settlements in California*, p 34.

12. Carrothers, p 154; Taylor, p 109.

13. Catherine Parr Traill, *The Canadian Settler's Guide*, p 31.

14. *Ibid*, p 33.

15. Taylor, p 114.

16. *Ibid*, p 164.

17. Traill, p 9.

Chapter 3
Grass Valley, California

T he baby was christened Selina Bice. Born on August 15, 1853, she was the daughter of Nicholas Bice and his wife Rebecca; the Nevada County Historical Society calls her "the first white child born in Grass Valley." More significantly, both her father and mother were born in Cornwall: Nicholas in 1818 and Rebecca in 1821. Thus the presence of Cornish families, as opposed to simply the presence of Cornish miners, is established almost at the beginning of the history of Grass Valley.

Grass Valley was already a bustling little town when Selina was born. The *Golden Era*, a San Francisco newspaper, stated in its edition of August 31, 1853:

> Grass Valley is indeed a lovely as well as a picturesque and very healthy town, business is lively here and the village can boast of good water and as handsome groves as any location in the State. The Miners too are averaging well throughout the section. Quartz mining is the most important business here as it embraces more capital than all other enterprises put together. The mills appear to be doing a fair business at present and several new ones are being built, the latter mostly by English capitalists.

In four short years since the gold rush of 1849 it appears that an economically viable community had been founded, but more than this, Grass Valley was emphatically a "respectable" community. The *Grass Valley Telegraph* of September 22, 1853, described a "moral and peaceful village . . . here we find many highly respectable families who have selected this as their permanent home; and these of course have thrown all their influence in favor of virtue."

That these words could be written at a time when most mining towns were hardly respectable communities is an indication of the values and aspirations of even the earliest settlers.

The history of Grass Valley is also, of course, the history of gold mining in California. T. A. Rickard tells us: "the discovery

Map 4. California cities and mining towns.

of gold in California by Marshall in 1848 was the most portentous event in the history of modern mining because it gave an immediate stimulus to world wide migration."[1]

News of the gold rush had also reached the Cornish mining communities in Wisconsin, Michigan and Jo Daviess County, Illinois. Men from these communities poured into California, traveling by the long and hazardous overland route. Most of these men intended to return to the Midwest and buy small farms. In 1847 over 700 people left Camborne for the Australian and American copper fields, and in 1849, when news of the gold rush reached Cornwall, a record number of over 1,000 people left Plymouth for Quebec in a single week.[2] It is reasonable to presume that a good many of these were Cornish miners who made their way down to California.

During those first gold rush days, anyone with a pick and shovel and a washbasin could hope to find gold. Later improvements to mining techniques included devices to aid in the washing of gold such as cradles (boxes on rockers), "long toms" and sluice boxes. Nevertheless, early gold mining was remarkably similar to the streaming techniques that the "Old Men" in Cornwall had used for tin. It was inevitable that one of the Cornish miners would have thought about digging into the quartz veins, and John Roberts himself seems to have had that idea, remarking that "the veins are formed exactly like the copper lodes in Cornwall, only they lie very flat."[3]

Apparently Roberts never carried out his plan, for the first discovery of gold in the quartz veins at Grass Valley seems to have been made by George McKnight and/or three other prospectors who were camping on a hill above Boston Ravine. These men, however, were ignorant of the nature of quartz ledges and did not know how to work them. They laid out square surface claims and simply dug up the ore and pounded it with hand mortars. Even so, they reported a yield of $500 a ton.[4] The news of their find was carried in the *Sacramento Transcript* and repeated in the *California Daily Courier* of San Francisco on December 5, 1850:

By recent information we learn that discoveries have been

made at Grass Valley of an immense vein of quartz, which bears gold so strongly that good wages have been made by men with a common hammer, who broke up the rock and picked out the gold in lumps varying in value from a bit to one dollar. The quartz bears gold so strongly that many miners have deserted old claims and located new ones in this vein.

The new quartz lodes required more sophisticated techniques in the form of mining machinery. John C. Frémont is generally given credit for bringing such machinery from England to California, and, at the manufacturer's suggestion, he engaged a crew of Cornish who understood how to operate the equipment.[5] But Frémont's machinery was to be used at his own Mariposa ranch. The first machinery in Grass Valley was installed in 1851 at the Stockton Mill in Boston Ravine by Halstead and Wright, who had brought it from Mexico.[6]

The demographics of Grass Valley tell the rest of the story. In 1851 there were only two cabins; on November 10, 1853, according to the newly established *Grass Valley Telegraph*, there were 200, and R. A. Eddy had published a map of the town based on a survey made by California Surveyor-General William M. Eddy. By this time Grass Valley had been described as a "moral village," and the Methodist Episcopal Church had been founded with 12 members.

On November 24, 1853, the *Grass Valley Telegraph* carried a notice about the "Ladies Sewing Circle" meeting at the Methodist Church; by this date there had been families with children living in the valley for well over a year, many of whom were Cornish. We know that Nicholas and Rebecca Bice had arrived in 1852, and in that same year Frances Strongman, her son Charles, her daughters Catherine Kelley and Elizabeth Langdon, together with their husbands, Enoch Kelley and Joseph Langdon, had traveled overland from Mineral Point, Wisconsin, to California. John and Frances Coad, with 5-year-old Frances Jane and year-old Laura, also went from Mineral Point to California in 1852, but they traveled via Panama.[7]

Further evidence of the Cornish presence is derived from

Grass Valley in 1852

local newspapers. The *Grass Valley Telegraph* of January 1, 1854, listed the names of those for whom letters were being held at the post office. We note an Estabrook, a Pasco and a Tregilyn, all good Cornish names. From the advertisements we learn that James Fenno was selling and repairing watches and jewelry, while Charles Retalleck advertised: "Horseshoeing done in the best and most durable manner. Mining tools repaired at short notice." On Christmas Day 1853 William Moyle married Carolyn Edwards, and while she may have been Welsh, he most certainly was a Cornishman.

By 1858 the pattern of life in Grass Valley was well established. The *Nevada National* (successor to the *Grass Valley Telegraph*) described the town on October 16, 1858:

> Neat cottages are springing up in the hills around, which with yards and gardens surrounded by handsome fences, with windmills for irrigation, show that the population here are determined to "live at home and board at the same house."

The reference is to the changed way of life of the miners sequential to the arrival of families in the town. The earliest miners had stayed in "hotels" or boarding houses, sleeping rolled up in a blanket on the floor. The boarding houses persist in the census records for another 30 years, but once the families arrived, even unmarried Cornishmen usually tried as soon as possible to find a room in a private house.

Much of the town of Grass Valley was destroyed by fire in 1855, but by October 9, 1858, the newspaper boasted businesses with "fireproof stores and storehouses." Those stores were supplied by mule teams with all the comforts the American economy of that time could produce and the miner could be persuaded to pay for. There was now a school with 412 children (210 boys, 202 girls), and a private school for "young ladies."

The Emmanuel Episcopal Church had been established in 1855 and a building, which still stands, had been erected in 1858. The Methodists, meeting in a building constructed in 1854, counted 65 members in 1858. There are many Cornish names in the church records, including Berryman, Rodda and Penberthy.

However, as in every age, there were setbacks. By the late

Grass Valley's Emmanuel Episcopal Church as it looked in 1895.

The Grass Valley
Methodist Church
in the early 1900s.

1850s a serious depression settled on the northern mines and lasted well into the 1860s. Some of the men left for other mining areas, including Fraser River in British Columbia, and the silver mines in Nevada. Some families left, but others stayed behind and waited for better times. In 1858 John Coad's letters to Fanny, who had returned to Wisconsin, mention that digging was very poor, wages only $3.00 a day and that it took $3 to $4 a day for a family to survive.

Frustration and poverty drove some Grass Valley residents to crime. In 1859 John Coad wrote, "There has been plenty robberies in Grass Valley and Nevada [City]. They have robbed so little as two bits and 3 pickaxxes." A gang of eight had robbed a store on Bear River in Placer County, then retreated to French Ravine in Grass Valley. The local sheriff and four citizens tracked them to the site, where crossfire killed two of the bandits and wounded another; one man with the sheriff suffered an arm wound.

Nevertheless, even in hard times, there were good times too. One of John Coad's letters mentions a "grand Ball and supper" sponsored by the Episcopalians and held in "a new house built on Church Street." The event raised $1,000 to support the new church. In April 1859 Coad wrote about another ball, this time in neighboring Nevada City. On this occasion 22 or 23 Grass Valley residents boarded the stage for the trip and "just before they got to the bridge going in to Nevada, there was a low place on one side of the stage, and in passing this place the stage turned over, and the way the crinoline or hoops had to suffer you must judge for yourself." However, in spite of a few bruises and the broken hoops, everyone managed to enjoy themselves at the ball where "there were 24 sets danced at one time."

The Cornish loved to celebrate; when news was received of the laying of the Atlantic cable, rockets were set off at Grass Valley, barrels and torches were lit, and 151 guns were fired! The Fourth of July was always a big event. In 1870 the Nevada City *Daily Transcript* mentions decorations that included young cedars cut down to shade the sidewalks; the paper expressed alarm at the waste. The Fourth was also the occasion for a great picnic with games for the children, band performances, and Cornish wrestling matches.

Even the schoolchildren's simple donations of food and firewood for the needy became the occasion for a pre-Christmas parade. That first parade was such a success that more time was given to getting together a bigger band the second year, and the Grass Valley *Union* advertised that "all musicians who can blow a horn or beat a drum" were invited. After the second parade the town band took over the job of leading the parade.

In addition to the town band, the Methodist Church band and the Salvation Army band, there were a number of other instrumental groups that played for concerts, parades and funerals. The pages of the newspaper during the first weeks of July 1893 contain heated comment in the "Letters" column. It seems there had been some competition between the bands at the funeral of Sheriff William H. Pascoe. It was said that "one band drowned out the other," and the members of one band accused the other of "playing unsuitable music."

Love of choral music was brought by the Cornish miners from their home country, and Grass Valley provided plenty of opportunity for this type of musical activity. Not only was there the famous Carol Choir, which sang at Christmas, but the miners had a choir of their own, and other groups were formed for special occasions. The *Union* of July 1, 1893, reported a "Grand Chorus of Male Voices" would take part in the Fourth of July celebrations.

The Miners' Union (later the Mineworkers' Protective League) not only was the representative unit for mineworkers, but also served as a benevolent and social organization. Every year there was a Miners' Picnic. A poster for this event in the archives of the Nevada County Historical Society advertises a Labor Day picnic at Olympia Park, midway between Grass Valley and Nevada City. The poster states that "all stores will be closed for the occasion," and residents of Grass Valley were invited to take part in "Tug of War, Cornish Wrestling and Races including a Fat Man's Race, a Fat Woman's Race, Shoveling Contests and a Ladies' Drilling Contest." Prizes of $2 or

$2.50 were offered. There was also to be an orchestra and an evening dance ("Admission 50¢. Ladies Free."). The general admission for the daytime events was 25 cents.

The reference to Cornish wrestling is especially interesting, because popularity of this ancient and unique sport, which to the uninitiated resembles both wrestling and Judo, had been declining in Cornwall itself. (Later the efforts of the Cornish Wrestling Association revived the sport.) In Grass Valley, however, the newspaper accounts of various meets with teams from all over Nevada County show the sport was alive and vigorous; one more demonstration of the maintenance of "Cornishness" into the second and third generation.

The 1895 Grass Valley Band, Harry Green Conductor. Members included William Bray, John Angove, Fred Morrish, Richard Goldsworthy, Richard Jewell, A. Hooper, William Winn, Bert Morrish, John Buckett, Thomas Tredrea, Fred Rowe, W. J. Martin (Secretary), I. Nicholas, John Pedler, A. Twitchell, Richard Angove (President), Charles Kerskeys, Fred O'Brien, Nelson Stevens and Charles Pascoe.

That there were many civic associations in the Grass Valley of the 1890s is clear from the contemporary press. One of the most important was the Sons of St. George, which restricted membership to those of English ancestry. According to the *Union* of July 1893, there 37 lodges of this organization with a total membership of more than 2,000 in California, Oregon, Washington, Utah, Montana, Nevada and British Columbia. These were all locations where substantial mining operations had attracted English emigrants. Representatives of 25 of these lodges met in a first "Grand Lodge Convention" at Grass Valley in June 1893, and William C. George was elected Grand President.

Other civic organizations active in the 1890s included the Independent Order of Odd Fellows and the Ancient Order of Foresters, both of which had been founded in England and subsequently developed American organizations. These were not only social clubs, but they also served the working men as important providers of life insurance benefits.

This then was the town to which so many Cornish families came. That most came to stay is clear from the lists of those who became U.S. citizens. In 1868, according to newspapers of the time, 358 Grass Valley residents were naturalized, 131 of whom were from England. In July 1869 at least 9 Cornish names appear on the list of new citizens, and in August the newspapers listed at least 22 with typically Cornish names (including Polglase, Temby, Paul, Northey, Samuel, Rule, Bawden and Prisk). This steady stream of new emigrants from Cornwall continued until 1954, when, with the closing of the Empire Mine, gold mining ceased at Grass Valley. However, the Methodist Church's biannual Cornish Fair, the ready availability of excellent Cornish pasties in stores, bars and restaurants, and the number of Cornish names still listed in the local telephone directory give testimony to the continuing Cornish presence in Nevada County.

NOTES

1. T. A. Rickard, *A History of American Mining*, p 20.
2. William S. Shepperson, *British Immigrants to North America*, p 83.
3. A. L. Rouse, *The Cousin Jacks*, p 246.
4. Doris E. Foley, "Another First for Nevada City, Part II," p 2.
5. Elmer E. Stevens, "The Cornish Miner," p 1.
6. Harry Wells et al, *History of Nevada County, California*, p 187.
7. Shirley Ewart, "Cornish Miners in Grass Valley," pp 40–45.

Chapter 4
The George Family

The George family provides a rich insight into the emigration pattern of some of the first Cornish immigrants to the Grass Valley area. John George, born in 1814 in St. Austell and his brother Samuel, born in 1819 in the same town, were the sons of Samuel George, born in 1748 in the parish of Roche. John married Sophia Clemo, and by 1848 the couple had three children. His brother Samuel was also married and had children, including a son, William C. George, born in 1840.

In 1847 the younger Samuel George immigrated to America; family tradition says he came to California, but possibly he first spent a period in the Midwest. We know he was in California by 1852 and had found work in the gold mines of Nevada County. In 1858 Samuel wrote to his brother John, suggesting he join him in Forest City in Sierra County, and urged him to bring Samuel's son, William C. George, now a lad of 18.

In that same year John, William, and a party of four others left St. Austell for America. William's diary records the voyage:

Monday morning July 18, 1858. I was up at 3 a.m.—got my luggage all safely packed—things seemed just as usual. The time will never be forgotten when I took the last look at Mother, Bro. and sister, they were in tears. I parted with all my friends, Uncle John in pretty good spirits. We arrived in Plymouth Station about half past 8 a.m. Changed trains and off to Bristol where we stopped for the night.

At 7 a.m. 19th of July we took a train to Liverpool. We slept on board that night and left the shores of Old England about noon on the 20th of July on board the "Kangaroo".

21st. My head is very light. Felt a little sick. I have to go down to get my boots because my slippers are too thin. I am so sick in consequence of an offensive smell below that I cannot see Queenstown, where we are at. I only spewed once.

22nd. Day spent on forecastle in singing, talking and I feel about well.

24th Sunday. I attended Divine Service in the Saloon, the

Captain read the Church of England form. Beef duff and potatoes for dinner.

25th. At 4 p.m. we are aroused by the jib breaking loose, women screaming and almost scared to death, but no damage done or danger.

26th. Stormy—spent the day writing and playing drafts. Not making but 27 miles an hour.

August 3rd. Arrived in New York—all are gazing on the delightful scenery on each side of us. About 9 a.m. we landed in Castle Garden depot, took a good wash in the free baths and engaged our lodging at the Western Railway house. I soon found out the Bank where I had to cash my Bill of Exchange, and had good luck. The dollars and cents seemed very strange, but I soon was able to use them.

4th. Up at 5 to see the sights—lost ourselves on our way home. As to describe New York—it is much like any other city—streets dirty and badly paved, the lower class is in abundance—swearing and cussing, cheating and whoring, gambling in full daylight. A Dutchman told me that the people of New York go about all day cheating each other. However there are also many good institutions and good Christians.

5th. We bought provisions and took our luggage down to the boat to be boarded. The steerage was so crowded that we could not get below and if we had not sheltered ourselves, we would have been dripping wet. I slept very little this night.

6th. Everything was a scene of bustle and confusion as we were estimated to be about 800 passengers about that small, ill ventilated, miserable boat.

7th. Sunday. No Divine Service so Uncle John, William Hoskin and myself got together just on our berths. This is the worst Sabbath I have ever experienced. We were afraid of putting into Havannah [sic] because the yellow fever was raging there.

9th. Some excitement today—a crazy man jumped overboard to catch a flying fish.

10th. We are off the coast of Florida

11th. Sailing off the coast of Cuba—the high mountains are very visible to us—very hot weather.

12th. Making 246 miles per day—more comfortable because we have left Cuba.

15th. Land ahead at day break—arrived in Aspinwall about 6 a.m. This is a thriving place with many white people but the majority are coloured. The Black children run naked but grown persons wear some kind of cotton covering. About noon we arrived in Panama by [rail] car. We took the tugboat out to the ship "The Golden Age .

16th. Laid off the coast of South America visible all day.

17th. Beautiful weather, the sea is like a small mill pool so smooth.

20th. Heard a sermon on "What shall I do to be saved?"

22nd. Crossing the Gulf of Calif. Making 283 miles a day.

Sunday 28th. We are ashore. Found it very cold coming up the Bay of San Francisco.

29th. Preparing for the mines. Walked and saw all we could in the time we had and about 4 p.m. went aboard the "Antelope" for Sacramento. This voyage seemed about as uncomfortable as any. We are on the deck—cold as winter and no overcoats to keep us warm. We got into Sacramento about 6 a.m. of the 30th. Paid 16.00 stage fare to Forest City and traveled as far as Nevada City.

31st. Started early—got to San Juan about noon—took dinner and waited hours for the stage. We left—crowded to excess. Had to walk some of the hills. Arrived in Forest City about 11 p.m. Met Father—but he did not recognize me. I was taller than him. We were all full of joy to see each other.[1]

Both men went to work with Samuel George in a gold mine at Forest City, which is northeast of Grass Valley in neighboring Sierra County. Their free time was spent panning for gold in nearby creeks, and William noted that many times they found nuggets weighing from 11 to 36 ounces. As fervent Methodists, they also took part in church meetings. Eight weeks after his arrival in Forest City, John George became very sick. William wrote in his diary:

October 25, 1858. Came home early from the mine. Tended Uncle John.

26th. I went to fetch mustard to make a plaster for him.

27th. Uncle thought he was much better but died suddenly at 9 p.m. He left a wife and [eight] children to bewail his loss.

The local Methodist preacher, Mr. J. H. Maddux, wrote this obituary about John George:

> Died of inflamation of the lungs in Forest City, October 27, 1858, Brother John George, a native of England, age 46 years. Brother John was born again in 1834 and has ever since been a member of the Methodist Episcopal Church. He came to this State only about eight weeks ago, immediately connected himself with the M.E. church of this place and was seldom absent from the prayer and class meetings and frequently testified to the power of that grace which proved to be his consolation in the hour of death. His illness lasted about eight days during which time he suffered much but without complaint. I visited him before his death and conversed with him in regard to his hopes beyond the grave. He said he had long been living in reference to a dying hour and he now believed that hour had come, but it found him ready. He talked so calmly and freely that I, fearing it would be too much labor for him, told him he had better not talk any more, but he continued to speak of his confidence in Christ and with emphasis repeated the following verses: "Forever here my rest shall be, close to they bleeding side. This all my home and all my plan, for me the Savior died." His death was emphatically that of peace. He leaves a wife and eight children in England to whom it remains to bear the sad news of his death. They will mourn, but not as those who have no hope.   J. H. Maddux, Forest City, Oct. 31, 1858.

Less than a month after John George died, his widow Sophia gave birth to their ninth child, Walter.

The modern reader must note the Cornish attitude to death and the equanimity with which John met his death, for death was no stranger to the Cornish miner. Such was the toll from accident and silicosis that John, at 46, was a man who had lived at least two years past the average life expectancy.

In 1865, six years after John's death, the family records that John's 22-year-old son, Samuel T., came to America to join his Uncle Samuel and cousin William in Grass Valley. How long he stayed is a matter of conjecture, but a notation in the register of the Grass Valley Methodist Church shows him as "removed" in 1868.

The same register records that on January 1, 1866, William C. George married Mary Ann Kitto. "Samuel George, Sr." was a witness, along with "Dr. George, Sol Kinsey, Mrs. Weeks, Miss Northey and a large number of others." The registrar goes on to note: "A grand 'charavari' after and the buggy broke down besides." The "Dr. George" is probably Dr. Richard George, listed in the 1870 census of Grass Valley as a physician, age 26, born in England. His wife, Mary W., age 25 was also English-born, and his two children, Lilly and Richard, were born in the state of Nevada. His relationship to the George family is unclear.

The 1870 Grass Valley census lists William C. George (retail grocer), wife Mary Ann, and child Clara (age 3). The same census shows Samuel George, now 51 years old, living in a Grass Valley hotel. Although Samuel had said he intended to send for his family as soon as possible, his wife and other children never did join him in California.

The next member of the George family to emigrate was John's second son, William H. (the cousin of William C.). On November 12, 1872, accompanied by his brothers, John and Samuel (the latter having decided to return to Grass Valley), 26-year-old William H. departed from St. Austell. Like his father before him, he left behind a pregnant wife. After he was gone, Louisa Ann (Jewell) George gave birth to their first child, named William Thomas, but usually called "Will T."

Thirteen long years later Louisa and Will T. left Cornwall for California. Perhaps it took that long before her husband became established in Grass Valley, but we also know it was hard for Mr. and Mrs. Jewell to part with their daughter and grandson, and they must have had reservations about her making the long voyage. Long afterwards, Louisa recalled her father telling her, "Now my dear, you don't have to go if you don't want to." She must have been torn between her love and devotion to her parents and her feelings of duty towards the husband that she had not seen for so long. All through the years, Louisa had faithfully written to William H., sending him the photographs which are still carefully preserved in her own gold-tooled brown leather album; the brass lock is testimony to their value. We see the curly-haired baby, Will T., first in a white dress with bows carefully hand-colored dark blue, and later in a velvet dress, smart with big pearl buttons. At 4 or 5 the boy is shown in a manly hands-in-pockets pose, wearing a sailor blouse with mid-length breeches. A little later he is photographed in a rather oversized overcoat that looks home-tailored—could it have been one of Papa's, cut down to size? Finally, there is the schoolboy, very much more grownup in cap and suit.

Louisa was a good mother, and concern about her growing lad's future must have been an important factor in her decision to join her husband. As for Will T., he had no reservations at all. In 1885 Louisa Jewell George

Will T., age 11, in St. Austell.

and her 12-year-old son left St. Austell with her husband's sister, Sophie Frost and Sophie's daughter Beatie; the Frost family would be joining Sophie's husband in New York.

The journey by ship and railroad must have been tremendously exciting for the boy. He treated the whole trip as a marvelous adventure and he, too, kept a diary to tell about it.[2]

October 6, 1885. Left St. Austell in the morning. It was raining. Got to Bristol where we stayed with Aunt Polly Jewell. Aunt Polly and Mrs. Pierce went as far as Bath with us. We took the train. Had to change cars at Didcot and again at Oxford. At Birkenhead the Liverpool Hotel man met us. Crossed the Mersey and took a cab to hotel. Wagon took the luggage.

October 7. Left for Docks. Wagon took the luggage. 12 o'clock went on board boat. Reached "City of Rome"—largest ship on the Atlantic run, too large to come in to docks.

Will T. went on to marvel at the fact that the ship was lit by electricity. The first day out they were still in the Mersey River and Will was congratulating himself on being a good sailor—but directly they reached the open sea it was a very different matter; the boy was very sick. He wrote:

October 7. Rough—sick

October 12. Sickness passed. Queenstown, Ireland. Rough and foggy.

October 13. Mother felt better. All classes of people on board; English, Americans, Germans, French, Irish, Scots, Dutch, Welsh and Jews. Cold, hail and snow.

October 14. Smoother—warmer.

October 15. Pilot boarded to take us into the harbor.

October 16. 5 a.m. Land. Passed Long Island light. Sunny day. Crossed the bar after a wait.

The party was thrown immediately into the bustle of New York City. They had to find their boxes, and unrope them to be searched by the customs official, who Will characterized as "a kind man—but thorough." The baggage had then to be reroped, a procedure with which they had "a terrible time." Then they all went to the Hamilton Parks Hotel for two days of sightseeing. This included a ride over the Brooklyn Bridge by rail. Aunt Sophie and Cousin Beatie then went on to their new home in New York, and Will T. and his mother crossed the river to board their train for the first lap of their journey to California.

Will described the train as being uncomfortable. They had to change at Pittsburgh. At 5 p.m. the train stopped for the passengers to get refreshments. The diary continues:

October 19. 6 a.m. Chicago. This is a very large city but

only 60 years ago there were only 3 Indian huts. Now it contains streets miles long. Part of it burned down 12 years ago, but all rebuilt and the city is growing rapidly. Five hours off again.

The journey across the United States was tiresome. They had to change trains once more at Council Bluffs, Iowa, and again there was the nuisance of collecting all their luggage and getting it onto the proper train for California. The weather was cold ("hard frost"), and once settled in their seats the boy observed and noted the scenery. He was excited to see prairie dogs, which stood upright in the fields, ignoring the train. He saw some wild horses being corralled—this was cowboy country indeed! On the evening of October 21 the train started the long climb up the Eastern slope of the Rockies. One engine broke down, which delayed them. Will T. remarked on the beautiful scenery and the snow on the mountains.

At Ogden, Utah, both climate and terrain changed again, and the two travelers found it "hot, sultry and dusty." Finally, at 4 o'clock on the morning of Saturday, October 24, 1885, Will T. and his mother reached the small station at Colfax, California where they boarded the Nevada County Narrow Gauge Railroad passenger car to Grass Valley. They arrived at their destination at 10 a.m. "Uncle John George was at the station. We were soon at his home, glad to be at journey's end," wrote the young diarist. The journey had taken Will T. and his mother only 18 days, compared with the 6 weeks required to travel from Cornwall to Grass Valley when his grandfather and his father's cousin, Will C. George, had come in 1858.

One can only guess at the joy with which, after so many years, Louisa and William H. George greeted each other, but William must have found it hard at first to cope with the reality of a teenage son. The lad from Cornwall for the first time met his Uncle John, now working as a blacksmith, Uncle Samuel T., a miner, and Great-Uncle Samuel, also a miner. The family stayed with Uncle John. There was also, of course, a whole host of cousins and second cousins, all about the same age.

During that first year Will T. attended school, where his

heavy Cornish accent caused some amusement. Years later he told his daughter: "I soon dropped my accent when I got to school here because everyone made fun of me."

One event during that first year in California made a lifelong impression on the young man. Shortly after he arrived in Grass Valley he was one of four teenage boys chosen to lead the first Donation Day parade, and he left his own account of that historic occasion:

It was in the month of December, 1883 that Mrs. Carolyn Hansen, a semi-invalid sitting at her window watching the children going to school, conceived the idea. What a help it would be to the needy persons of the city if every school child on the last day of school before Christmas brought to the schoolhouse one stick of stove wood and one potato.

The school trustees and teachers picked up the idea. For four or five years all school children would go to school carrying donations. Then Theodore Wilhels suggested the parade, and since parades were expected to be headed by a band, for that first Donation Day parade, a band of four teen-agers was pressed into service. This consisted of Charles and Robert Van Loan, the sons of the Salvation Army Captain; one boy played the cornet, John J. Stevens, father of Elmer Stevens, on the bass drum, and Will T. George on the snare drum.

Many of the schoolboys, not content to carry a fourteen-inch piece of stove wood, bravely lugged along a stick of four foot wood—and Ma and Pa had to sacrifice the largest stick of wood from the winter's supply. And of course the largest potato in the family kitchen was sought out to be given to the poor. The girls in the parade were also equal to the occasion and carried stove wood and potatoes or packages of food, canned goods, etc. . . . Not forgetting the businessmen's part in the parade, which followed along with the school children. This section represented almost every line of business in the city: butcher, baker, grocer man, dry goods man, and cord-wood by the truck followed the parade.

Employees of business houses formed a section of the parade carrying blankets, sacks of flour, canned goods, vegetables, meats, poultry, and strings of sausages, some of these in comical arrangements. Others had little bags at the end of

Participants gather to form an early Donation Day parade on School Street near Neal, in front of what had been Grass Valley's first "Advanced Grammar" (High) School, which was a few steps away from the home of Carolyn Hansen, who inspired the event. After the Columbus School was built in 1892, the building became the Lincoln School for elementary grades, and it continued to be used for various educational purposes until 1938.

sticks. I recall one in particular where the late Judge Paynter had his little sack of money dangling from a fishing pole.

The first parade was such a success that more time was given to getting together a bigger band the second year, and the *Union* advertised that "all musicians who can blow a horn or beat a drum" were invited. After the second parade the Grass Valley Town Band took over the job of leading the parade.

The next year, at age 14, Will T. went to work in the mines. A picture taken in 1887 shows him dressed in his work clothes and standing a little apart from the bearded miners, but looking quite composed. He was a good-looking lad and he retained these good looks all his life.

William H. and Louisa picked up their life together during the next few years. In 1886, a year after her arrival in Grass Valley, Louisa gave birth to a second son, Frederick John, and then in 1888, Harold Jewell was born. Edwin Gladstone arrived in 1890. With four healthy sons it would seem that the family was prospering, but in 1891 tragedy struck. First, baby Eddie died of pneumonia, and then, three months after the funeral, 4-year-old Freddie was wading in the creek when he slipped and fell, hitting his head. A mastoid infection followed and within hours the boy was dead.

The following year must have been difficult for poor Louisa. We know from what her son told his own daughter Lucille that she was most desperately homesick; she must have been terribly heartsick as well. In 1893 things took a turn for the better when Horace Radford was born. He was always called Ray, and his arrival after such a sad interlude must have been like a ray of light to the 44-year-old Louisa and her 47-year-old husband. In that same year William's cousin, William C. George, was elected to his first term as mayor of Grass Valley.

In 1894 Louisa was able to return to Cornwall with Harold and baby Ray and Will T., now a young man of 21. They took with them Will's cousin Albert, son of William C. The family did not stay away for long, but while Louisa and the children stayed in Cornwall, Will T. and Albert toured England and France. Lucille Simons remarked later, "After they came back,

The Grass Valley residence of William C. George at the corner of Colfax and South Auburn streets.

William C. George during his tenure as Mayor of Grass Valley.

Grandma was satisfied—and never wanted to go back to England again."

William T. George, carpenter, age 23, and Annie J. Edwards, age 19, were married on May 27, 1896. The register of the Grass Valley Methodist Church records that his second-cousin, Albert G. George, was a witness along with Miss Laura Tippett. Annie was a miner's daughter, of Welsh stock but born in Vermont and raised in Michigan and Grass Valley. The photograph in Mrs. Simon's collection shows a sturdy little person with a clear, direct gaze. The back of the photo is inscribed: "New Instantaneous Gelatin Bromide Process. At Eureka Gallery, Mill St. by W. A. Clinch, Artist Photographer."

On May 25, 1897, Lottie Eileen George was born; her baptism is recorded on August 18, 1897, at the Methodist Church. A son, Elton Frederick, followed in January 1900, and in 1902 Evelyn Lucille (the Lucille Simons of this history) joined the family.

It was shortly after this that Will T. decided to go into business for himself as a painter and decorator. First he bought out a general store, and then, to increase his income, he opened

Will T. George and customers.

paint and wallpaper departments. A picture of the store in the early 1900s shows him standing proudly by the counter. In the background are neat racks of paint and wallpaper, while beside the counter is a display of picture frame moldings; his daughter remembered the beautiful carved gilt frames.

The life of the George family, like the lives of the majority of Grass Valley's Cornish population, centered around the Methodist

Church. Will T.'s father, William H., was a lay preacher, and by 1893 he was also assistant superintendent of the Sunday School. On Sunday there was the church service, and all the boys sang in the choir as soon as they were old enough. After the Sabbath dinner there was Sunday School. There were also meetings of church societies, such as the Epworth League and the Ladies' Aid (Sewing Circle), and special events like revivals, some of which lasted as long as five or six weeks. The big annual United Sunday School picnic was a treat involving a ride on the narrow gauge railroad out to Shebley's Pond near Chicago Park. The children especially loved this outing, which must have been a rough ride, since the "seating" on the railroad flat cars consisted of unplaned 2x12 boards!

For the Georges, as for most Cornish families, religion was not just a Sunday affair. The rules of the church prohibited dancing and theatergoing, as well as card playing, and, of course, drinking. The Sabbath was a strict day of rest. Lucille George Simons remembered that on Saturday night the sewing machine was closed up and all the children's toys were put away. However, the Will T. George family was more liberal than the previous generation, and Lucille was allowed to play with her paper dolls on Sundays. The big meal was Saturday dinner; on Sunday a light lunch was served when everyone returned from church. After dinner came Sunday School, and in the evening there would be another church service. In addition, Epworth League meetings were held before church for the teenaged members of the family.

The Salvation Army provided another outlet for the family energy, both religious and musical. William H. George preached for the Army on Saturday nights, and at various times the boys played in the Salvation Army band. Music was very important to the whole family. Lucille Simons described Will T. as "a great musician." He could play the piano "by ear," and he also played the cornet and both alto and bass horn. Much later he learned to play the banjo and the violin.

Will T.'s interest in music brought a new invention to Grass Valley. An advertisement in *The Daily Morning Union* of

Will T. George with Lucille and Lottie in his store about 1910. The Victor dog (on counter at right) listens for "His Master's Voice."

January 6, 1907, advised the reader that "W. T. George has been appointed agent for the Columbia Talking Machine and Records." A 1910 photo shows Lottie and Lucille standing with their dad between huge lily horns of the machines. By then Will T. also sold competing products, because the photo shows a display of the dog listening to "His Master's Voice," the trademark of the Victor Talking Machine Company. Lucille recalled that the records for these machines were cylindrical.[3]

Will T.'s affairs were thriving. He built a fine residence on Neal Street, about two blocks from his father's house. It was close enough to see the spire of the Methodist Church and Lucille Simons recalled, "Dad painted the church steeple himself; he wouldn't tell Mam when he was going to do it, but we could see him from the porch of our house."

In an age when family discipline was often harsh, Lucille remarked that "We knew [Dad] meant what he said, although he never spanked us girls." Her memories are of a warm, fun-loving man:

> When Dad was home, we'd beg him: "Come on Dad, sing songs," and he would get out the banjo or the violin and play and sing for us. At Christmas there would always be a big crowd, then Dad would play and sing comic songs. We'd all

laugh at one song I remember, it was called "The Laughing Song." I remember Mrs. James laughing until she was in tears. Then we'd all get around the big dining room table to play games like "Simon Says Thumbs Up," or "Hunt the Thimble" or card games like "Flinch."

The red-letter days were Donation Day, which was still about the way her father had recalled it, and the Fourth of July. A picture of Will T. in 1920 shows him in his first car. The open Dodge touring car is decorated for the parade with five American flags, and, not to slight his English roots, one little Union Jack on the radiator. Red, white and blue bunting covers the hood and the wheels are decorated with red, white and blue flowers. The owner is sitting there looking pleased as Punch.

Family picnics were great occasions. Lucille Simons recalled:

> Sometimes we'd ride the streetcar that went to Nevada City, but we'd get off at Brunswick Road and walk to Olympia Park carrying a picnic basket. There was a lake there, with an island in the center that had a dance floor. We'd swim in the lake.

Lucille remembered the climate as being colder in Grass Valley in those days; there seemed to have been more snow and the children had fun sliding and sledding. Young Lucille attended Grant School and Bell Hill School and later Columbus School, as did all those children in Grass Valley who were not Catholics. She recalled little poverty in those days, saying, "most children dressed pretty well." The largest group of children were of Cornish ancestry, although by Lucille's day most were American-born, but there were also children of Irish and of German parentage. She said there were a few "colored" and some Chinese.

There were Chinese laundries, and Mr. Tin Loy, who had a vegetable garden, came round the houses with two baskets of vegetables slung on a long pole over his shoulder. "Chinatown" was just down the street, and the George children would look through the fence and watch as the Chinese roasted pig for a feast.

After 1906 life was definitely happier for Will T.'s parents in the new home William H. had built for his family on Neal Street. (His grandson, Harold T. George, lives there now, and one can still admire the workmanship of the beautiful hand-planed moldings around the doors.) In 1912 William H. George died, leaving Louisa alone with Harold J. and Ray in the house on Neal Street.

After the boys grew up, Louisa's sister, Polly Jewell Broad, came from Cornwall to keep Louisa company. Aunt Polly worked in Bert's millinery and dry goods store in town and Lucille described Grandma and Aunt Polly as jolly old ladies who enjoyed each other's company. Then, in 1927, Polly died, and once again Louisa was alone.

Cindy Guinn Ward said her great-grandmother Louisa was a little person, less than five feet tall, who seldom went to town but did go to church. Louisa's commitment to her religious beliefs was absolute, but church was not just a religious experience, it was also her only social outlet and she enjoyed being included in the "Old Ladies Tea." She seems to have

The "Old Ladies' Tea" at the Grass Valley Methodist Church, ca 1914.

grown old gracefully. April 1st was her birthday and she liked to say: "My dear, I'm just an old April Fool." The family would tease her about her age—and she loved it! She lived to be almost 85 years old.

Harold Jewell George, born in 1888, was 15 years younger than his brother Will T. He was the "middle child" who had been 3 years old when his older brother Freddie and younger brother Eddie had died in 1891. Harold left school after the 8th grade and for the next 4 years he was apprenticed to Will T. as a painter and decorator. He was paid 75 cents a day and the older brother did not spare the 13-year-old. In later years Harold told his own son that he walked as much as three miles to work, carrying scaffold and ladder all the way. In those days they made their own wallpaper paste from flour and water, and in the winter the weather was so cold the paste would freeze.

The lad learned the important thing was doing the job right: "If it only took an extra hour to finish a job right, the extra hour would be spent, and no extra pay demanded." When Will T. suffered lead poisoning and could no longer work with paint, Harold took over the job of painting the church steeple. He also was responsible for installing the cross on top of the spire, a feat others had called impossible.

Harold George shared the family love of music. Will T. had a cornet, and when the boy expressed an interest in the instrument, Will T. told him that he could have it if he could learn to play it. In a very short time Harold had mastered the cornet well enough to play in a band formed mostly of young fellows from the Methodist Church. He then learned to play other instruments, including the flute, and some years later, the saxophone. By the time he was 16 he had become the leader of the "Star and Crescent Band."

Soon the young man was persuaded to join other musicians who played for dancing on Saturday nights. This association caused some problems between the generations because his father ("Old William") maintained that dancing was "of the devil." To make matters worse, the dances might go on after midnight and into the wee hours of the Sabbath, and band

Grass Valley Concert Band. Ray George (middle of back row), Melvin Angove (2nd from left in middle row), Fred E. Nettle (6th in middle row), Harold J. George (seated 2nd from left), Will T. George (seated on far right).

The Grass Valley Concert Band 1916-17. L to R starting at top: ROW 1: Fred E. Nettell (1st trombone), Lester J. Richards (2nd trombone), E. L. Bosquit (1st trombone), O. L. Twitchell (G. trombone), A. M. Angove (bass), Lorin Kemp (bass), L. W. Hooper (B.B. bass); ROW 2: John Monahan (euphonium), Jack Kitchen (tenor), Ray George (alto), John Bradley (1st alto), Ed Curnow (alto), Billie Winn (solo alto), John E. "Jack" Nettell (1st cornet); ROW 3: Edward B. Paynter (sax), Leland V. Michell (clarinet), Joseph Ducotey (2nd clarinet), Tom Wills (soprano cornet), James Andrews (1st cornet), Frank Colvin (2nd cornet); ROW 4: Walter Hyatt (snare drum), Prof. H. W. Hooper (leader), Harold J. George (solo cornet), Will T. George (2nd cornet), Norton Penrose (bass drum). Boy in background unidentified.

rehearsals were held on Sunday afternoons; the old folks did not approve. Most of the teenagers who had played together in the Star and Crescent Band eventually joined the Grass Valley Concert Band. In the Video Museum of the Nevada County Historical Society in Grass Valley is a photograph of the members of this band in 1916. The photo shows a young, slim and very intense Harold J. George, solo cornet. He is standing next to the slightly heavier and mustachioed Will T. George, 2nd cornet. Will looks quite relaxed. Younger brother Ray, who played melophone, is also included in the photo. At that time the band was led by Professor H. W. Hooper. Eventually, Harold became director of this band, and he remained its leader for over 40 years.

Cindy Guinn Ward said about her grandfather Harold, who was called "Papa" by all his grandchildren:

> Bands were popular in the era before the automobile age and Grass Valley was famous for its park and for the bandstand where Papa would direct a concert every Saturday night during the warm months.

Harold George loved the tradition of music, and especially the choral music that was part of the Cornish heritage. He is quoted as saying: "Whenever two Cousin Jacks get together, one of them is bound to suggest: 'Let's 'ave a bit of 'ark 'ark!'"

On October 9, 1915, Harold married Nellie Thomas, who was of Welsh descent. Harold T., was born on May 15, 1920 and daughter Carol Marie on October 9, 1926. For his family, Harold built the house on Neal Street next door to the home his father had built. Harold T. was born in this house, but Carol was born in Jones Memorial Hospital.

In the early 1920s Harold became the director of the Grass Valley Carol Choir, a group with which he had sung since boyhood. His son, Harold T. George, recollected that the days before Christmas were literally filled with song. On the Sunday before Christmas carols were sung during the morning service of the Methodist Church, and in the afternoon the choir would sing at the County Hospital in Nevada City, the Jones Memorial Hospital in Grass Valley, and on to the homes of housebound former members of the choir. In the evening they again sang at the Methodist Church, and then on to the Salvation Army—the whole day would be spent singing. On Christmas Eve, rain or shine, the choir sang from the steps of the Union Building. Those in the back were sheltered under the building's overhang, but when it was storming poor Harold J. was out in the open, conducting.

Reflecting on her childhood, Carol George Guinn realized how much "Cornishness" was preserved. Her father retained the food preferences of his own father. Kippered cod was cooked in a brown paper bag for Sunday breakfast, and Christmas pudding was made each holiday season. Liver and onions was also a frequently served dish, perhaps because it was so typically English, or maybe just because the butcher gave away liver for free! The kitchen had two gas burners, but most food was cooked over the wood fire or in the oven of the wood stove, and Harold J. had a special preference for cake that had "fallen," which was bound to happen if anyone opened the oven door while the cake was baking. He was not above instigating the collapse of his wife's cakes!

For several years Harold pursued his trade as a painter and decorator, and he followed the example of his own older brother and took his young brother Ray as his apprentice. Some time after his marriage, however, he decided to change his trade. His granddaughter Cindy records that "he and his brother Ray opened a shoe store on the southwest corner of Mill and Main Street. 'The Bootery' furnished the miners with their boots and their ladies with stylish 'needle nose' shoes." During World War I the store was sold and the brothers returned to the painting and decorating trade and operated a small paint and decorating store nearly opposite the library.

About 1928 Harold decided once again to change direction. He got together with a friend, Caleb Chinn, and opened "The Harmony Shop," a music store where they not only sold music and musical instruments but also gave music lessons. As an incentive for their grade-school students, they started a "Boys' Band," a military-style band that played for the Fourth of July

Harold J. George directs the Grass Valley Carol Choir at the 2000 foot level of the Idaho Maryland Mine. Men in back: Elmer Lewis, Gerald Pratt, (unknown), Oakley Johns, (unknown), "Scotty" Partington, Bill Tremewan, and M. Henry Argall. Boys in front: (unknown), Howard Phillips, (unknown), and Melvin Hamilton.

The Gold Miners Chorus (a sub-group, not actually part of the Carol Choir) also sang from underground during the Christmas 1940 broadcast. Left to right: Harold Hansen, Oakley Johns, "Scotty" Partington, Fred Clemo, Bill Tremewan, Bill Bartle, and Ed Burtner.

parade, which by this time alternated between Grass Valley and Nevada City. The boys wore white shirts and pants and sailor hats, and Grass Valley folks cheered them as they marched by.

Harold's obvious rapport with children, his teaching ability, and the enthusiasm of his young students impressed the Grass Valley School Board, which suggested another new venture: a music program for the elementary and high schools. The school board hired Harold part time, even though he had never attended high school; however, shortly before he started teaching, he received a special music teaching credential from the state. He then offered his services to Nevada City, and soon he was teaching four schools a day in the two towns. After this first year he taught full time in Grass Valley.

Harold attended the summer program for music teachers at San Francisco State College; he also learned to play stringed instruments and started a string program in the schools. His career as a music teacher lasted 18 years and ended in 1948 when his son, Harold T., became the music teacher at Grass Valley High School.

Harold J. George continued conducting the Grass Valley Carol Choir, an all-male choir in the Cornish fashion. The boys sang the alto parts while the first tenors carried the melody; the second tenors and the large bass section carried the harmony. During the 1930s and 1940s the choir traveled to San Francisco, Sacramento and other nearby cities, and to several hospitals in the Napa Valley. On their yearly trip to the San Francisco Bay Area, the Grass Valley Carol Choir broadcast typically Cornish Christmas Carols over local radio stations.

The itinerary would be to leave Grass Valley at 5 a.m. by Greyhound Bus to San Francisco, where they would sing at several churches. At noon, with two dollars each to spend, the choir ate lunch at Fisherman's Wharf, and sang at the afternoon service at Shattuck Avenue Methodist Church in Oakland, where many members were former Grass Valley residents of Cornish descent. After a Cornish pasty dinner, the choir would sing again at the evening service and then leave for home at nine in the evening; a long day for people who had to get up very early Monday morning to go to work.

In 1940 the Grass Valley Carol Choir performed on the NBC radio network from the 2,000-foot level of the Idaho Maryland Mine. The Christmas carols were rebroadcast on the "Death Valley Days" western adventure radio series in 1941 and 1942, and in 1946 the choir broadcast a Christmas concert live from the stage of Grass Valley's Del Oro Theater.

In 1950, at the behest of the National Folklore Society and the Library of Congress, the choir made a tape recording of the carols and history of the group as a permanent record of the activities of Cornish pioneers in America. Later a high-fidelity recording of 12 Cornish carols was made at the Grass Valley Methodist Church, which had been given a fine new organ by Simon L. Crase, son-in-law of William C. George and a long-time member of the choir. The record enjoyed a small commercial success and the president of the Grass Valley Chamber of Commerce was appreciative: "Harold George has done plenty to put the town on the map, he has given us national and international publicity."

Carol Guinn and her daughter Cathy discussed Harold's values. They said he respected education and was an avid reader with omnivorous tastes. He continued to read extensively until his eyesight failed. In a speech, Harold expressed his ideas on the sort of education young people should have: "Citizenship should be taught as a subject from kindergarten through college. Youngsters at the start and at the finish should be taught that others have their rights too."

During the ensuing years, Harold J. George was thrice elected a member of the high school board of trustees, serving a total of 12 years. In April 1965 he was named Citizen of the Year by the Nevada County Historical Society for his contribution to music, and was named "Nevada County's Music Man." His son, Harold T., said this was probably the proudest moment in his father's life.

The Native Daughters of the Golden West planted a red

maple tree and erected a marker in his honor, explaining at the presentation: "Mr. George is not a qualified native daughter, but he exemplifies the ideals of our parlor."

Harold Jewell George died suddenly on January 23, 1973, just short of his 85th birthday.

NOTES

1. Cindy Guinn Ward, the granddaughter of Harold Jewell George, provided this account.
2. The writer is indebted to Will T. George's daughter, Lucille Simons, who in 1979 shared her memories of her father, along with his diary.
3. In the first years of the 20th century, the Victor Talking Machine Company manufactured disks and Edison made only cylinders, but for a time Columbia was making both disks and cylinders.

Chapter 5
The Henwood Family

Both John Henwood and his wife Jane Prior Henwood were born in 1828 in St. Blazey, Cornwall. We know little about John, but Jane appears to have been both impulsive and strong minded. Perhaps life at home was boring for this high spirited girl. Although she rarely talked about her native land, she did tell one story to her granddaughter, Loretta Henwood Trathen, which indicates her temperament:

> My grandmother told me that they used to have a vegetable garden, and in that garden there was one exceptionally large cabbage. Every time grandma saw that cabbage she had a feeling that she must cut it, why she didn't know. One morning she got up at five o'clock, took a kitchen knife, cut the cabbage and let it roll away down the hill. It settled all the way down the street at the crossroads, and no one in the neighborhood ever knew how or why that big cabbage ever got there.

John Henwood and Jane Prior Henwood had seven children. Josiah, Loretta's father, was their fifth child and was born in 1858. Once again, we are aware of the pressure that must have resulted from supporting this large family. Old Crinnis Mine, once one of the most productive in Cornwall, had been abandoned in 1818, and the St. Blazey area had been generally depressed since then. It seems clear that, for John, economic factors must have been paramount. Jane, we know, enjoyed dressing well and living well, and she must have abetted her husband's desire to improve the family fortune, but the romantic idea of immigrating to the New World may also have influenced her, appealing to her imagination and to her sense of adventure.

In 1873 John Henwood and his wife, Jane Prior Henwood, decided to join the flood of immigrants to the United States. Their son Josiah was about 15 when the family, including all seven children, embarked on the steamship *Boston* for America.

Fore Street in St. Blazey in the early 1900s.

This was the last voyage of the *Boston*, which sank on its return trip to England.

The family was too poor to make the journey all the way to California, although this was to be their ultimate destination. They landed in New York, and years later Jane still remembered her fascination with the lights of the metropolis. Then they went to Cold Spring, on the east bank of the Hudson River, in Putnam County, New York. Here the whole family worked, although what their employment was has not been recorded. They saved their money and were soon able to move to Freeland, Pennsylvania, in the heart of the anthracite mining region. Here again they worked and saved, and within a relatively short time they were able to fulfill John's ambition to travel to California. On September 9, 1875, John and Jane and their children arrived in Grass Valley, having traveled across the continent by train, and from Colfax on the little narrow gauge railroad.

All the Henwood men went to work in the mines. We know little of the first years of Josiah Henwood's life in California, but in 1894, when he was 35, he married Ida Luke, born in Grass Valley, a 21-year-old daughter of Cornish parents. Their first child, daughter Loretta, was born the following year. Eventually there would be five other children.

Loretta Henwood Trathen shared her memories of growing up in Grass Valley before World War I. Her father Josiah was a hard-worker whose values were education, patriotism and religion. Like his parents, he had been illiterate when he left Cornwall, but he taught himself to read, and his daughter said "he wrote a beautiful hand." Josiah was proud that he could figure sums in his head and called himself "a ready reckoner."

Although he never ran for office, Josiah was interested in politics, and never missed a city council meeting. In the evening after supper he would join other Cornish men downtown and they would sit and talk politics.

Loretta declared, "We were all born Republicans" adding, "a few of us have changed—I don't know why!" She recalled, "We were raised on the *San Francisco Chronicle*, we were not allowed the [San Francisco] *Examiner*—and Papa read the newspaper from cover to cover."

After Loretta was born, Josiah bought a $1,000 bond, a tremendous achievement for a man who earned only $3 a day. This was for his daughter's education. He used the interest, but the principal was handed to her intact to pay her college tuition, and she remembered: "Papa lived for the day I would go to college—even when things were hard, he never touched my bond."

In 1900, lured by the promise of $5 a day, Josiah went to Wardner, near Kellogg, Idaho. A tunnel was being dug to connect the Bunker Hill and the Sullivan mines. Josiah took charge of the timbering crew, but he returned to Grass Valley after a year because there was no provision for his children's education in rural Idaho. He always considered his family in all his work assignments; he worked as a pump man and as a timber man, but would never do drilling because, "I have six children at home and I want to live to raise them."

Later he worked at the curiously named W.Y.O.D. Mine ("Work Your Own Diggings") and the 3,500-foot-deep Empire Mine, where the subterranean levels extended for miles. Before

1907 the miners worked a 12-hour day; they never saw daylight, and their children were often in bed before the fathers returned from work. It was not until the strike of 1907 that the 8-hour day was introduced.

Josiah was always conscious of the ever-present risk of death or dismemberment in his occupation. Later in life he was given the task of "breaking in" young miners during their first weeks on the job. He often expressed himself as heartsick at having to introduce them to such a hazardous calling. When Loretta's future husband, Will Trathen, came to work at the Empire, Josiah said, "Taking him underground was one of the hardest things to do." He had known Will all his life.

Loretta characterized her father as "the greatest American citizen—he could not find one thing wrong with this country, and he thought those born here took America for granted." Josiah had become naturalized as soon as eligible, but his daughter recalled that for some other Cornish becoming citizens might not have been entirely their own idea. It seems a well-known local politician of Cornish ancestry was running for the state assembly. He needed all the votes he could get, so he loaded all the Cornish men onto the narrow gauge railroad to Nevada City and had them all naturalized!

Asked about the relationship between her parents, Loretta described it as warm. Josiah always brought his whole paycheck home to his wife. She in turn would see that his clothes were kept in order, and she always shined his shoes. She was not, however, permitted to mend his underwear; a proud man, Josiah would not go to work in patched underclothing!

Josiah, like the other miners, carried his lunch pail every working day. The tea was put in the bottom, and then the meat, packed separately from the bread, which would be on top. When the pail was heated, the tea would be good and hot, and that would heat the meat, but Josiah hated warm bread. Later he got to like coffee and would ask for that instead of tea.

Meals in the Henwood house were substantial: plenty of good homemade bread with butter and jam for breakfast, and on Sunday mornings there was usually codfish. Papa liked rice

Hard-rock miners with candles and a lunch bucket.

pudding and insisted that he be served it for dessert every day, but there would often be tapioca or sago pudding as well. All work for the Sunday dinner was completed on Saturday, although the dinner itself would be cooked on Sunday morning and served at about 12:30 when the family came home from church. There was usually a roast with potatoes and another vegetable, and always on Sunday there were two desserts. Loretta remembered:

> Grandpa [John] Henwood and Grandma [Jane] Henwood separated when I was about ten. I don't know their trouble. Grandma moved to a little house on the hillside, while Grandpa lived in a kind of lean-to cabin on North Auburn Street. Every Sunday my father insisted we take [Grandpa] his Sunday dinner. Mother had a linen cloth with matching napkins, and we wore the napkins out taking him the dinner. He probably had enough food for a week.

On Sunday afternoon, after Sunday School, the whole family would come home for Sunday tea with bread spread with cream and jam or with cream and "golden syrup."

Mrs. Trathen has few memories of her grandfather, John Henwood, and remarked, "we really never got to talk much." Of her other Henwood relatives, she best remembers her Uncle Jim, her father's brother. A lifelong bachelor, James Henwood had worked in Johannesburg, South Africa, and in British Columbia at Britannia Beach, which in those days was accessible only by boat. Jim loved history, and his niece recalled he had beautiful books on the presidents of the United States which he read and re-read. He also liked to tell risqué jokes which were met with stern frowns by Loretta's mother and his own sister Lizzie—until he had left the house and then they would both collapse with laughter.

Jane Prior Henwood seems to have relished life in America. Her granddaughter remembered her as an old lady who, when Loretta was little, lived two doors away. "I used to sneak away on Sunday to visit her, and she would be beautifully dressed in a beaded taffeta gown with a bonnet and cape." "G'wan 'ome,

Lorettie and tell your mother to dress 'ee up and we'll go to church," Jane would tell the child.

In 1979 Loretta still lived in what was once her grandmother's house, which provided graphic reinforcement for another memory. The backyard was clay, which extended under the house, and there still remained the indentations of the big pans of milk from Grandma's jersey cow. These pans were some two feet wide and would be set down overnight for the cream to rise. Loretta recalled:

> If there was enough milk, Grandma would make Cornish Cream. The pan would be put on the back end of the stove, it was there for hours. When it got to be glassy and wrinkly, Grandma knew it was done. She'd put the pan down in the cellar, and on the third day it was skimmed.

The skimmer was a handleless dessert-plate size metal disc with holes in it. Grandma's cream looked and tasted very different from the modern Cornish-made product that can be bought at dairies in Truro or St. Ives. It was very smooth and lacked the graininess of the English product.

After Jane Henwood separated from her husband, she moved to a little house on the hillside overlooking the town. There she had all her "treasures," including some figurines she had brought with her from England. Her granddaughter described her sitting on the porch on summer evenings. Below were the lights of the town and the spire of the Methodist Church, and Jane would say over and over again, "This is just like when we landed in New York!"

Jane Henwood never learned to read or write, and in her last years her sight failed. She would dictate letters to Loretta, who still recalled the address of Jane's sister Mary Anne at Parr Station, Saint Blazey, Cornwall. Mary Anne was also illiterate, and so the letters would be read to her, and she in turn would dictate a reply. Jane always hoped for a cure for her visual problems, and when salesmen from passing medicine shows came through town she would show them her eyes, and they would shake their heads and tell her she was "incurable." Loretta believes her grandmother probably had cataracts.

The old lady would feel her grandchildren to see how big they had grown, and the children were delighted to run errands for her, buying the 10 cents worth of fish that was sufficient for her dinner. In spite of being unable to see, Jane Prior Henwood lived to a very ripe old age.

Loretta Trathen was both a miner's daughter and the wife of a miner. I asked her about "highgrading." Was this ever discussed as she was growing up? Did the miners manage to smuggle gold out of the mines? Had any fortunes been founded on these ill-gotten gains? "Yes," she admitted, "some had."

> Papa was a timberman and timbermen went in first. When the timbering was done they left, and there was little chance for them to pick up ore. For those who were drilling, the opportunities were different; you can look around today and see men who couldn't have begun to save the money they have now on just what they earned in the mines!

But Josiah Henwood never made a great deal of money, and he died a poor man.

Chapter 6
The Bennallack Family

James Bennallack was a mine captain, who later became an owner of the Empire Mine in Grass Valley, as well as vice president of the Pacific Mutual Insurance Company. As such, he represents one of the most successful of the Cornish immigrants to Grass Valley.

The seventh of nine children of John and Jane Bennallack, James was born in Redruth, Cornwall in 1836. Like most Redruth men, James and his three surviving brothers, William, Mark and Joseph, were all miners. Although in the 1850s copper yields from the Cornish mines were reaching record tonnage, life for the miners had hardly improved. The Bennallacks, like so many others, realized that, for a better life it was essential to leave Cornwall. Like so many others, they crossed the Atlantic, landed in New York, and traveled by rail to Mineral Point, Wisconsin. However, according to the newspapers, the real opportunities were in California, where the quartz mines demanded Cornish workers who were skilled at blasting, and knowledgeable about using pumps in the mines and stamps to crush the ore above ground. By 1856 all three Bennallacks were in California.

James first worked in Sonora, in the southern Mother Lode, but almost immediately went back to Cornwall. After visiting his parents, he was set to return to the States when his older sister Catherine asked him for help. Her husband, miner Harry Trezise, had already emigrated, first to Virginia, and then overland to California. Catherine, who had a small baby, was anxious to join her husband, but had decided the sea route via Cape Horn would be easier than the long trip across the plains by covered wagon. She asked James to accompany her and help her on the voyage and he agreed.

The first part of their journey, the voyage across the Atlantic, was uneventful, but as their ship navigated the waters close to the Central American coast, it ran aground. Convinced the vessel would sink, Catherine tied 2-year-old Katie to the mast; however, passengers and crew were rescued and taken to Aspinwall. Faced with a long wait for another ship around the Horn, James and Catherine decided to walk across the Isthmus, accompanied by the inevitable mule for their baggage. On reaching the Pacific port of Panama, they were able to complete their voyage, first to San Francisco, and then up the Sacramento River. In 1856 Catherine joined her husband, probably in one of the Mother Lode towns, and James came to Grass Valley, where his brothers had settled.

In that same year James married Mary Rowe, who had been born in Redruth. During the next 22 years, James and Mary had 12 children, of whom only 6 survived to maturity; it almost seemed as if as soon as a new baby was born, another child died. These must have been truly anxious years for poor Mary, and if, as it was remembered, she rarely let her children out of the house, it is not hard to understand why. The neighbors remarked, "Mrs. Bennallack kept her babies like hot-house plants."

During these years James pursued his work as a miner, first as foreman of the New York Hill Mine, then as underground superintendent at the old French Lead Mine or North Star Mine where he installed new pumps, and with his brother uncovered the South Star Mine. In 1858, like many others from Grass Valley, he took part in the Fraser River gold rush and, like most others, was happy to get back home. He worked in several other mines, eventually becoming a superintendent or "captain"; he developed a reputation as a mining expert, which led to journeys to assay mines in Colorado, Idaho, Arizona, New Mexico, and Mexico, as well as Alaska, Montana, and Idaho. In 1880 he reopened the Sebastopol Mine, which had been idle for several years, using pumps and machinery from the idle Bullion Mine. The *Nevada County Mining Review* of August 1, 1895, said ". . . his judgment can be relied upon."

James thrived financially and built a fine house on Empire Street, where in 1878 his youngest son, Francis Williams Bennallack, was born. In 1885, when Francis was 7, the house

James Bennallack (above) and his residence (below).

burned down, but some furniture was rescued, including Mary Bennallack's rocking chair. Soon a new house was built, up-to-the-minute in every way, with one of the first bathrooms in Grass Valley. The house has been beautifully restored by James and Mary's granddaughter, Sibley Bennallack Hansen, and the bathroom still boasts its big tub, resplendent with oak rim.

Eventually James became a partner in the Empire Mine. During these years he went back to Cornwall at least twice, but Mary did not, probably because she refused to travel without her children and could not have taken all six. She did, however, keep in touch with her family, especially her sister, Priscilla Rowe Phillips, who lived in Camborne. Clearly, Mary enjoyed Cornish cooking; in a letter dated 1902, Priscilla mentions that she will soon mail some "saffern" (saffron), an essential for saffron buns.

Like most Cornish, Mary and James brought their family up according to strict Methodist tenets; Sunday was a day of rest, and all cooking was done on the Saturday. Sibley remembers her Aunt Allie as being aghast that the grandchildren were allowed to play cards on the Sabbath. James' relationship with the Methodists ended after he put a $20 gold piece in the collection and the preacher remarked that "the man who could afford to give $20 to the church, could certainly afford to give more!" Upset at this, he and Mary joined the Congregational Church, and remained members for the rest of their lives. James died in 1887 and Mary in 1905.

Mining was always a hazardous occupation. Two of James Bennallack's brothers, Mark (an underground superintendent) and Frank, had been killed in the Eureka mine. Nevertheless, James and Mary's sons, James Henry and Francis Williams (always called Frank) followed in their father's footsteps; James eventually became a captain at the Empire Mine. In 1905, while working in the powerhouse of the North Star Mine, Frank lost four fingers on his left hand. On his mother's deathbed he had slipped her wedding ring onto his little finger, and while greasing the large compressor at the mine, the ring caught in a cog and four of his fingers got pulled into the machinery. The wide

Gold miner using a single-hand drill in a stope at the Empire Mine.

wedding band prevented his hand from going in further, and his partner was able to stop the machine. Daughter Sibley writes: "My Dad had coal black hair before this happened," and he told her it was "salt and pepper" the day after the accident, and in three days was completely white. Frank's Uncle Joseph Bennallack also lost two fingers in a mining accident.

Frank was married twice, first to Annie Murray, from California's Napa Valley. They had one son, Francis James. Annie died in 1913, and five years later Frank married schoolteacher Susan Harrigan. Susan was of English-Irish descent and was related to Rudyard Kipling. Their oldest daughter Sibley was named for Susan's mother. There were two sons, Brian and Bret, and another daughter, Iris.

In spite of the fact that her mother was not of Cornish stock, Sibley feels the household she was brought up in was very Cornish in its orientation. Her father was proud of being Cornish, and his wife and daughters learned to make pasties. Perhaps as a concession to Susan, coffee was served for breakfast, but there was always tea with lunch and dinner. And father insisted on what he said was a Cornish custom: Milk had to be poured from the *front* of the pitcher, never from the side!

Since the next-door neighbors were also Cornish, the children, including Sibley, all played soccer. Music was important in the Bennallack household. Frank loved to sing, but Sibley regrets that somehow musical ability was not passed down to her; however, she does play in the handbell choir at church.

Education was also important. Frank served on the Grass Valley school board for 12 years, from 1937 to 1949. It was not the custom in those days to employ married teachers, and the wife of a school board member would not ordinarily have been allowed to teach in that district, but when the male teachers were drafted during World War II, Susan (formerly a successful teacher in one-room schools at both Rough and Ready and Mariposa) returned to the classroom. She continued to teach at Grass Valley even after she was past the normal retirement age of 65.

Today her daughter Sibley, happily married to Arlie Hansen (the son of a Danish emigrant), preserves her Cornish heritage as carefully as she takes care of her grandmother's beautiful house.

When asked to define "Cornish Values," Sibley replied quickly. Honesty, certainly; people were expected to deal honestly with each other in business as well as in personal relations. Although "highgrading" might have been tolerated by some, it was considered a disgrace by people like the Bennallacks

According to Sibley, the most important Cornish value was concern for other people. The Cornish of Grass Valley cared about people and they looked after each other. Stories of old James Bennallack describe his compassion and concern for anyone injured under his supervision; when Minnie Chinn Farley's father was ill, she remembers that James Henry Bennallack (son of "Old James") always came to their home to see if anything was needed. This tradition is a fine legacy; one that, it seems, the people of Grass Valley have kept alive.

Chapter 7
The Chinn Family

S amuel George Chinn, usually called by his middle name, was born in the village of Penponds, Cornwall, in 1870. In 1882 George's parents and a brother died in an epidemic of the "Black Plague," and the 12-year-old was left head of the family. He had to help support his younger brother Caleb and sister Mary Ann. George Chinn immediately left school and went to work in the mine. The boy was so small he was carried up and down to the working levels on the back of an older miner.

At the age of 17 George set sail for America at the suggestion of his maternal uncle, George Richards. By joining his uncle in the gold mines of California he hoped to make enough money to raise his brother and sister and give them better chances in life. Nine years later he was able to return to Cornwall, where he met and married Katie Treloar, daughter of Benjamin and Catherine (Ivey) Treloar. Benjamin was a farmer and he also owned the Roseworthy Flour Mill, so by contemporary standards the family was well off; however, there were 17 children.

In later life Katie emphasized that, unlike other parents of the time, Benjamin never forced his boys to follow in his footsteps; each child was given a chance to choose his own occupation, and there may have been no pressure on Katie to accept the hand of the young miner. We do know her parents approved of the match, and we also know, from subsequent events, that relations between Katie and her mother were apt at times to be strained. Katie must have been in love with George Chinn, and she may also have wanted to get away from her domineering mother and the large family. It is certain that, even if her family had felt some economic strain, this would not have been the primary reason that brought her to California.

Samuel George Chinn and Katie Treloar were married in 1896, and George brought his bride back to Grass Valley the same year. He had been living in California for nine years and was well established, but Katie had no relatives in the States and must have been most miserably homesick. Her daughter, Minnie Chinn Farley, recalls the story as it was told to her many years later. "Mama would cry to go home, but there was no money for Papa to go with her, and she wouldn't go by herself."

One day, after a particularly tearful session, George Chinn told his wife: "Back you're going to your mother." He took out the steamer trunk she had brought with her, and started pulling her clothes out of the closet. "Did you have this when I married you?" If she said "Yes," he threw the dress aside, saying, "I can't send you back in old clothes!"

As the new American-bought clothes piled up on the bed, Katie melted. "I can't go, I don't want to go," she pleaded. And she stayed. The first years were not happy though. Her first baby died "in utero," and surgery was necessary. For five years after this experience she remained sickly, confined to a wheel-chair, and for many more years she suffered from "epileptic fits," that may have been the result of her desperate unhappiness.

In 1902, fully 13 years after their marriage, George and Katie became the parents of Minnie. The birth was difficult, and the baby, though not premature, was very small. But Minnie survived, and one can only imagine the joy this baby must have brought into her parents' lives. At that time the family was living at Jackson in Amador County, but soon they moved back to Grass Valley. As it appeared Minnie would be an only child, little Caleb, named for George's brother, was brought into the Chinn home to be raised with her.

It does seem that Katie remained homesick, and in 1905, after receiving news that Minnie's grandmother was ailing, all four Chinns went back to England. The welcome Katie received seems somewhat mixed. Baby Minnie was "boarded out" with a retired nanny by the name of Henrietta (Hetty) Hawkins. Minnie said she felt that as "the American child" she was not considered worthy of living in the Treloar house at Roseworthy, but one wonders if George Chinn's relatively humble background might have contributed to Mrs. Treloar's rejection of her 3-year-old granddaughter; or was it simply an invalid's feeling that two children in the house would be disturbing?

Almost immediately on arrival in Cornwall, George Chinn took off for Johannesburg, where Cornish miners were in great demand in the gold mines. However, the trip was short: George became sick on the ship, and as soon as he reached South Africa he boarded another vessel and came right back to Roseworthy. He had lost so much weight that Jane did not recognize him. Later, George described South Africa as a place where miners had only a "butterfly life." Men still in their thirties would develop "miner's con," the emphysema that left them crippled. "They earned good money—but they didn't have the breath to walk." Things were not all that much better in Cornwall. Minnie recounted how the lads came up from underground "looking as if they'd been in a flour mill."

Although she was very young at the time, Minnie had no trouble remembering her two-year stay in Cornwall. Hetty was kind to her, and Minnie kept in touch with her until her death. One day Hetty took the child to Falmouth and there, at the top of the "Jacob's Ladder" steps the woman met, by assignment, a man who kissed her. Minnie told her mother about the event and Katie was duly shocked; she had not realized that Hetty had "a follower."

The relationship with Grandma Treloar remained prickly. Minnie remembered:

> Mam buttered bread for Caleb and me, and Grandma said: "Fancy putting butter on bread, you can't afford that!" Mama said she could, and Grandma asked, "Suppose their father died?" Mama then said, "Well then, let them have it while he's alive!" ... Grandma wanted Mama to scrub the granite gate posts at the entrance to the driveway and Mama refused.

Katie began to believe life in California was, in retrospect, much more congenial.

George did well in his remaining year in Cornwall. He became a "tributer," working with a gang of men under contract to Dolcoath mine. Minnie recalled:

After the hole has been drilled and the blasting powder inserted and tamped in place, a miner lights the fuse with his candle and then retreats to what he hopes will be a safe distance to await the result.

At that time they did not use dynamite in Cornish mines, but Dad had a blasting certificate from California, and he told the men: "If you'll go along with me, maybe we'll make some money." They struck it good and made money, but Dad wanted to get back to America, and after Grandma died in 1907 we all came back. We were all glad to be home. We came in on the old narrow gauge and stayed with Dad's aunt, Mrs. Weeks.

The family found a little house that rented for $10 a month, but there was still not much money, since at that time George Chinn earned only $2.25 a day. Nevertheless, life in Grass Valley was, as Minnie remembered it, very pleasant. When Minnie was about 10 years old a dramatic improvement occurred in her mother's health. Both Katie and George had become alarmed by the frequency and severity of Katie's "epileptic" bouts, and finally "my mother and father prayed all night by the side of the bed, and she never had another spell."

A photograph of the family taken at about this time shows the children: Caleb a little stolid, Minnie pretty and impish. There is Samuel George Chinn, the respectable and solid *pater familias*. However, Katie is the surprise—this picture does not match the image of a delicate invalid. She is a beautiful young woman, with gaily dancing eyes, and there is a strong resemblance between her and her young daughter.

Minnie remembered her mother as a good cook and homemaker. "I never came home but what there was bread or cake baking." It did seem as if people were more neighborly then. When someone was sick the neighbors would help.

> Mrs. McCleod was sick with T.B. [tuberculosis] and the neighbors took her children and raised them, and Mam went out and begged money to add a room to the McCleod's house so that when she recovered she would have a separate room for her children.

When other neighbors were sick, some of the 10 or 12 loaves a week Mama baked would be set aside for the neighbor's family. Later Caleb kept up the practice, sometimes baking 6 to 8 loaves a day. "When my Dad was sick, the neighbors came and sawed wood for our stove." Nevertheless, Minnie was quick to add that people preferred to be independent when at all possible.

Life for the family of a miner was always precarious. This was before the days of the Mineworkers' League, and when someone was hurt or disabled in the mines there was no compensation; the wife would simply have to take in boarders, do laundry, or hire out to work in domestic service in order to raise her children. The dust in the mines was bad, and almost all miners had some degree of "miners con." Later the formation of the Mineworkers' League did provide some measure of compensation: $1.00 a day for injuries and $100 if the man died.

Before the 1907 strike the hours were appallingly long; the children hardly saw their father when they were little. "He went to work before dawn and when he came home they were in bed." For these reasons, when the men did strike they had the full support of their wives: "Mama would not urge my father to return to work."

Minnie expressed both love and admiration for her father: "He was a prince of a man. He was the same all the time, and he was good to everyone; he gave away everything he ever had." She added that not all miners were that exemplary; some who had wives and children in Cornwall remarried in America and never gave another thought to their first families.

George Chinn was a staunch Methodist, and like quite a few other Methodists of those days, he was also associated with the Salvation Army, with which he used to preach on street corners. Minnie described her father, who had left school at 12, as largely self-educated and, like other Cornish, a self-taught musician:

"Give him any instrument and he'd play it: cornet, concertina, accordion, organ," Minnie remembered. "Every Saturday night, Dad took us to town to the dance hall to watch people dancing." Minnie herself never danced, saying with a smile, "I hadn't any music at all!"

Minnie and Caleb went to the Grant School, located at Winchester and Marshall streets. One teacher, Matilda Stevens, was especially memorable. She was "about six feet three tall," and she ruled her classroom with a big, black strap. One time a boy put three mice into Minnie's desk. When she opened her desk she screamed and was promptly banished to the hall for causing a disturbance, until the teacher herself saw the cause of the commotion.

Minnie liked school, especially when "Dad used to bring our lunches over, he'd bring us hot chocolate when it was snowing." But she had less pleasant memories of the sanitary facilities: "We had outdoor toilets, four holes. The stink and the flies—boy it was awful!"

Electric power had come early to Grass Valley, so the Chinns had electricity for lighting, but not for cooking or heating. Life at home was often hard work. All water had to be boiled in a boiler, and then the dirty mine clothes were scrubbed on a washboard. This, plus the wear and tear from hard labor, made constant patching necessary. The Chinns did have an indoor toilet, but no bathroom. The family bathed in a tub set in front of the woodstove and filled with hot water from the boiler.

There were fun times too. "When the wood man brought the wood, we'd go out to Berryman's ranch on his wagon and get an apple, and then walk two miles back again." Sunday School picnics would be looked forward to for weeks, and on Labor Day all the stores would close and everyone would go to the Miners' Picnic. Minnie's mother would pack stuffed peppers and pasties, sandwiches and potato salad. Everything went into a big basket with a handle, to be taken on the narrow gauge railway to Shebley's Pond. The passengers sat in open-topped box cars, and once they got to the park there would be games and races. The children took part in sack races, wheelbarrow races, and egg and spoon races. The young people picked wildflowers, and there would be a prize for the prettiest bunch.

Minnie Chinn Farley remembers the wonderful parties; her father would move the woodstove out to the porch so the children and their guests would have more room to play in the house. And, of course, in the summer there would be hayrides: "They'd get a wagon full of hay, and everyone would climb up on top and go to Bear River for a picnic."

Picnic cars being pulled by Engine No. 5 of the narrow gauge railroad.

Donation Day was the big event just before Christmas:

> Boys used to carry a six-foot stick of wood or fifty pounds of potatoes. We used to take big things in those days, not just a can like they do today. And we'd march and the bands would all play. Oh, it was beautiful in those days! I remember Ed Bosanko with a hundred-pound bag of flour. The parade started at the Columbus School and went down Auburn Street and back Main and Mill Streets, and we'd drop off the goods at the Elks' corner, by School and Main. They don't enjoy themselves today like we used to do. When it was snowy they'd close off Main Street hill to Auburn Street and we'd slide down on sledges and toboggans and things.

Christmas meant plum pudding, and Mama's fruit cake, a recipe so good that later, after George Chinn died, Mama would bake it in coffee cans and sell it. The house was decorated with holly and mistletoe. Minnie recalled her mother telling her that when she had first come to America she had never heard of Santa Claus. Katie had gone to visit some friends and when Santa Claus "in person" walked in, the young woman from Cornwall nearly fainted at the apparition!

Grass Valley was a happy place in which to grow up. People paid attention to the niceties:

> The butcher would deliver to your door with an old wagon with all the flies around, but he would always give us a hunk of bologna, and liver and bones were given away for free. And the vegetables were sold by a Chinaman with two baskets on a long pole. The water bill was paid at the door to the water collector who made his rounds.

Thus community links were forged and maintained.

Students and teachers marching in the 1905 Donation Day parade.

Not only did the stores close on Sundays and holidays, but if there was a funeral all the stores pulled down their shades and closed their doors, and people on the street would stand at attention until the cortege had passed. There were no super-markets or all-purpose drug stores; grocery stores carried only groceries, meat markets sold meat, and pharmacies sold drugs and health aids.

In those days the stores were closed on Sundays, respecting the strict Sabbatarian tenet of the Cornish. Asked what broke this pattern, "Greediness," was Minnie's quick answer. "The chain stores coming in really was what brought the change. Safeway wouldn't close on Sunday." Minnie thought people who worked in the supermarkets were not happy when they found they had to work on Sundays.

Grass Valley seemed to Minnie to have been quite a homo-genous community: "Almost everyone was Cornish, but a few Chinese. . . . There were some Irish families, but they were down Boston Ravine." There was not much difference in the standard of living between the Cornish families. There were a few Cornish mine owners, but the top layer of wealth was really the merchants: Angove Clothing Store, Rowe, Harris. All the children, mining family or merchant family, went to public school. The Catholic convent was a boarding school and a business school in those years.

The Chinn family enjoyed hearty and plentiful meals. "Dad used to buy half a hog and pickle it," Minnie remembered. She also recalled "the fish man would come from Santa Cruz with pilchards. Mama would dry some on the clothesline and mari-nate some." A whole dried codfish was bought to be served for Sunday morning breakfast, or sometimes salted salmon bellies, or "bloaters" (smoked, unsplit herrings).

> The family drank tea, we never knew coffee. I don't ever remember hearing much about coffee when I was a kid, I don't know why, unless because Mama was English we al-ways had tea.

What about adolescence? What was it like being a teenager in Grass Valley in the 1900s?

Kids were more mature then. There was no junior high, you went straight to high school where you took either a three-year commercial course or a four-year academic course, but most of the boys went to work in the mine when they were 14. More girls than boys stayed on in school, but the graduating class was only about 25. At 13 I was working in George Tresize's variety store, and I was in charge of the store. I took care of it when the Tresizes were away. Even before that I would mend the butcher's clothes. After graduation most girls went to work, and a lot left Grass Valley and went to Sacramento.

Did any girls get pregnant before they got married? "Yes, some did, but their mother would raise the child as if it was their own." Minnie told of one mother who went so far as to pretend to be pregnant, and when the daughter, who had been sent out of town, had the baby, the mother made out as if it were her own.

When Minnie was 17 her mother got sick and the girl left school to look after her. Then, when her mother recovered, Minnie went to Armstrong Business College. After graduation she was employed at Bert George's Grocery store.

Bert George took me on to work in the office. I did all the bookkeeping, double entry, cashed all the checks. I got $40 a month and I was the highest-paid girl in Grass Valley.

In 1927 George Chinn became ill and in 1931 he died. He was just 60 years old. Minnie continued to live at home, enjoying life, and was in no hurry to get married. Four years later Cornishman Ed Farley came into her life and the two were married. Katie, however, was not left alone; she lived with the couple for 26 years until in her nineties she died.

The rest of Minnie's story is included in the life of Ed Farley in Chapter 11.

Chapter 8
The Rowe Family

They were married in 1900, and their daughter Winnifred Rowe Cannon still treasures their wedding picture. The groom, James Jenkin Rowe, has a sensitive face. He is good looking, with dark hair, a moustache, and lively dark eyes. His well-cut suit is obviously new and his shoes are shined to a high gloss, and as he waits for the camera to capture the moment, he is obviously and comfortably at ease. The bride, Alberta Peters, stands tall. She is a real beauty with dark hair piled high and decked with rosebuds. The long sleeves of her high-necked white dress are trimmed with rows of tiny tucks and Valenciennes lace. But it is her eyes that hold the viewer. Dark, steady, they look straight at the camera. One senses that this is a woman who knows what she wants—and very quietly gets it!

Cornish ambition had enabled this highly respectable couple to rise and take a place in Grass Valley society. Although both came from mining families, Jim had never been a miner, and Alberta had been well trained in the social graces needed by the young wife of an upwardly mobile husband. Their marriage was happy and lasted 61 years, but in spite of the Rowes and the Peters having a common Cornish background, the two families were as different as chalk and cheese.

Joel Rowe, father of the groom, was born in February 1845 in St. Agnes Parish in Cornwall. His granddaughter, Winnifred Cannon, recalls that he "never went to school a day in his life," which was not unusual for Cornish children before the establishment of National Schools. Like most other lads in Cornwall, he worked as a miner, and probably at a very early age.

The 22-year-old Joel married 19-year-old Mary Jenkin in May 1867. Soon after this he left Cornwall for the United States, leaving his bride behind. Joel wanted to be sure he was established before he brought Mary to the new country, but he must have returned to Cornwall at least once, and certainly was

Wedding photo of James Jenkin Rowe and Alberta Peters in 1900.

there by the fall of 1871. On June 1, 1872, in the parish of St. Allen near Truro, Mary gave birth to James Jenkin Rowe, named for her father. Shortly after his son's birth, Joel, now an American citizen, left Cornwall again. This time his destination was Grass Valley, but again Mary stayed in Cornwall. Joel wanted to be sure the California mining town was a respectable place before he sent for his family.

Baby Jim, an American citizen by right of his father's naturalization, was 11 months old when Mary finally left Cornwall to join her husband. The sea voyage took 14 days, and the rest of the journey another two weeks, but as far as San Francisco Mary was helped by the Harris family, members of a party of Cornish on their way to New Almaden, California.

By this time Mary's brother John already was in Grass Valley, and Joel was living with him. In 1877 the Rowe family left Grass Valley for Bodie, in eastern California, where Joel worked at the Syndicate Mine. Twenty years later, in 1897, James Rowe wrote:

> . . . my sister Syndie was born July 19, 1878. She being the first white child born at the Syndicate Mine, the people wanted her named Syndicate which she was and as a token of respect the people of the place gave her a baby buggy which cost eighty odd dollars. . . . When she was 1 year and five months old we left Bodie on account of so much sickness there.

Because by this time many other children had died, Joel packed his young family into a sleigh and they returned to Grass Valley. Here they stayed for just three months before leaving for Jackson, in Amador County. It was February 1880. The sickness the Rowes had escaped in Bodie followed them to Jackson. James' account continues:

> While we resided at Jackson, I came near passing in the checks. I had a severe attack of the scarlet fever and was not expected to again regain any health and I was unwell for a long time. Before this, I was a fat, plump boy but since I have been thin.

After just nine months in Jackson, the family returned to Grass Valley, where they stayed only six months before going to Calaveras County, where Joel bought three mines at West Point. Here both Jim and Syndie went to grade school. Jim later supplemented this early education with night schools at West Point and Grass Valley, and a home-study course for electricians.

In West Point Mary Rowe learned along with her children. When she and Joel were married, she had signed her name with an "x." Now she learned to read and write, although she always remained sensitive over her handwriting, and in later years she asked her granddaughter Winnifred to address envelopes for her. Like most Cornish of their generation, Joel and Mary expected their children to go farther in school than they had. Above all, they had no intention of Jim working as a miner. Winnifred remembers the old people saying they "didn't want their sons to be muckers."

Some time during these years, Mary Rowe's health started to fail, and she and Joel returned to Grass Valley, bought about two acres of land and built a house. Winnifred remembers the old couple as being steadfast Methodists. They would not even read the Sunday paper on the day it arrived—they had to wait till the Sabbath was over!

She remembers how particular they both were, especially over neatness and cleanliness. She was told that, when the couple lived in West Point, Mary was so worried over whether she was getting the sheets as clean as she should, that she would ask anyone going to San Andreas to buy a new white sheet, so it could be compared with her newly washed bed linen! Winnifred well remembers her grandfather's shop in Grass Valley. The floor was spotless and all the tools were lined up by size. Grandpa Joel, in spite of his lack of formal education, valued learning. On the kitchen table were two books, the Bible and the dictionary, and each was referred to frequently.

Mary Rowe, though never considered a great beauty, was a good-looking woman who dressed conservatively, always in black: black taffeta on Sundays, and black-and-white print calico in the summer. In the house she wore a "wrapper," a high-necked ankle-length dress made with long sleeves and no waist. To provide a waist, one tied on an apron. Mary quite often would wear three aprons over her wrapper, so she always had a clean one if unexpected company arrived.

The Rowes took pride in being Americans. Both had become naturalized citizens, and Joel voted regularly; like most Cornish he was a Republican (in contrast to Grass Valley's Irish, French and Italian residents, who were more apt to be Democrats).

In 1889 Joel had built a sawmill in West Point, and in 1895

he joined with partners to build a new and larger mill at Moke-lumne Hill. By this time young Jim was 17, and his father gave him the job of bookkeeper/foreman at West Point.

We are fortunate that Jim's daughter Winnifred has carefully preserved her father's diaries for 1897 and 1898. The entry for January 1, 1897, finds 25-year-old Jim working on the books for the lumber mill and mine. Joel and Mary had just arrived from Grass Valley, and in the evening they all visited Mary's brother, Tom Jenkin. The financial records occupied Jim's time most days, but often he was called on to help out in other ways. The sawmill had a steam-powered "donkey" engine, and Jim often helped stoke the two boilers.[1] He also spent entire days loading sugar pine lumber onto wagons that horses would pull all the way to Grass Valley.

It was not all work. On Saturdays Jim took pleasure in going out to the woods, where he shot squirrels, quail, and even an occasional robin. He also enjoyed fishing, and once recorded a catch of 25 fish.

Sunday was a day of rest. In Grass Valley, Jim, true to his Methodist upbringing, had never missed Sunday School nor the evening church service, and sometimes even attended morning service. But in West Point there was nowhere to go and nothing much to do. He missed the busy social life of a larger town, and several times he wrote in his diary that he was "lonesome."

Except for short periods with his parents at Grass Valley, Jim lived on what he proudly referred to as "my ranch," which was a 30-minute walk from the mill at West Point. To cut down on this travel time (and also, one suspects, for fun) he bought a bicycle. Apparently he needed practice riding it; after the first time out he recorded: "had a dickens of a time!"

In May his loneliness was somewhat assuaged. He and two Cornish friends, James Sampson and Henry Bunney, put up a telephone wire, and on May 31 he talked over the phone for the first time. The next day, June 1, was his birthday, and he went to the West Point schoolhouse to vote for school trustees.

In July 1897 Jim Rowe returned home for a vacation. His diary mentions he went alone to the Independence Day parade, then spent the evening with Alberta Peters, a neighbor and fellow Methodist. He must have enjoyed himself; the next day he wrote: "Took a walk with Miss Peters in evening. Had ice cream and cake." When he went back to West Point, Jim and Alberta carried on a busy correspondence, and within a month "Miss Peters" had become first "Alberta" and then "Bertie."

In September he saw bear tracks and two bears crossed the road near the mill. Tracks were laid for a railroad to carry logs to the mill; on September 30 he wrote: "2,000 feet of logs brought down over the rail. 6 horse teams." All this time his work was closely supervised by his father, who corresponded with Jim from Grass Valley and paid frequent visits to the mill.

Alberta Peters, his father, and his sister Syndie were Joel's only regular correspondents. On October 12 his sister married W. H. Rowe, also of Cornish descent, but not a relative. On her wedding day Jim wrote to his sister, saying he was "feeling very blue because I cannot be there. . . . I am now going to bed with a sad heart."

On December 9, 1897, Jim was once more back in Grass Valley. The very next day he records: "saw Bertie." On Sunday the couple took a walk together and then went to church in the evening. On Christmas Eve Bertie gave him a necktie and he presented her with a "gold breastpin in the shape of a leaf." (He kept careful accounts at the back of the diary, and the pin cost him $11.)

Jim reveled at being back in Grass Valley, where Christmas Day festivities included carol singing in the morning and a ball game in the afternoon. That evening he and Bertie went to a concert. The diary ends with a summary of the year, and we can clearly see the direction of young James Jenkin Rowe's ambitions:

> 1897 is now at an end and we are now to begin another year. . . . I have had a very pleasant time but I trust I shall have a pleasanter one this year as the last year I have been compelled to be away from home and folks. I have been an employ[ee] of the Eureka Mine and Lumber Co. of West Point, Calaveras County filling the position of bookkeeper and overseer and general knockabout. A very good job but long hours and no Sundays to rest and go to church and also

in a very desolate and lonesome place with only very rough and ill bred people to associate with—all they look for is something to eat and a place to lay their heads. Clothes and the like, they think nothing of, only enough to cover them. Mostly half breeds of some sort.

I am at present in Grass Valley, Nevada County, California which is home to me as I have lots of dear kind friends and a very nice place, lots of company and plenty of amusements. This is the best place on earth for me.

His declaration is signed with a flourish: "Respectfully, James J. Rowe." The diary ends with a biography, a record of books he read in the past year (and his opinions of them), and a few pages of accounts, which included $10 for a suit of clothes and 15 cents for a toothbrush. Other than his payments for board and lodging, the Christmas present for Bertie was far the most expensive single item Jim paid for during the year.

The diary for 1898 looks exactly the same as the little book used the previous year. Jim, still in Grass Valley, remarked that he attended the wedding of Alberta's sister, Clarinda (Clara) Peters, and E. Magor on New Year's Day. Bertie was a bridesmaid, and on the next day, Jim took a walk with Bertie after church.

The diary reports he rode his bike almost every day, and on January 4 went to a revival meeting. On the 5th he went duck hunting without success, but on the 6th he killed one duck and one hare. On January 21, happily unemployed at Grass Valley, he records: "Bummed as usual."

Perhaps Jim saw it as a last, wild, bachelor fling. On Sunday, January 23, Jim and his friend Fred Sleep boarded the narrow gauge train, bound for San Francisco. They witnessed a parade, visited Oakland, the Cliff House, Sutro Heights—and also Chinatown and the Golden Gate. Their tour of the city included the city jail, the Institute of Art, and the Academy of Science, as well as a ride to the wharf on a cable car and trips to Sausalito and Mount Tamalpais. In the evening they went to the Orpheum and the California theaters, as well as the Rivoli and Moscone's.

Church was not neglected: on Sunday morning Jim visited St.

Ignatius Catholic Church and in the evening worshiped at a Methodist church. He honed his technical education by visiting the Miners' Fair and the Union Iron Works. And finally he recorded the vacation by having his picture taken at a photographer's studio.

Jim left San Francisco on Wednesday, February 2. He had been gone for eleven exciting action-packed days. Returning to Grass Valley, he went to church that same evening and again on the very next night. There is no mention of Bertie until Sunday, when the couple enjoyed their usual walk and evening church service together.

The following week Jim's dental problems occupied his attention. On Monday his dentist filled four teeth, one with a temporary filling. For the next two days that tooth ached, and on Friday the dentist had to "kill the nerve" of the offending molar. The next week the dentist "pulled the nerve out of the tooth. I nearly fainted."

One mysterious entry is in code:

QDUDAKDE C MY KNWD SN GDQ.

It is hard to read the individual letters, but Jim's daughter Winnifred cracked the code, a simple transposition of letters:

REVEALED B MY LOVE TO HER.

Note that, in his excitement, Jim forgot to code "MY" or the letter "A"! Valentine's day brings bliss. Again the entry is in code, and decoded it reads: "Ask her to be my wife and she said she would." And then no code, just triumph: "Happy am I."

Jim's father had asked Jim to take charge of the lumber mill at Mokelumne Hill. This he agreed to do. So, with the prospect of leaving Grass Valley, and anxious to formalize his engagement, he bought a ring for Bertie and took it to her. In his diary he wrote: "She's the sweetest and best girl on earth to me. . . . I am very sorry I got to leave her but there may be a time when I should not have to." During the next month the diary reveals that his fiancee had acquired a new and even more intimate nickname: "Birdie."

Little of excitement was happening at Mokelumne Hill, but

it was more interesting than life at West Point. Here there were neighbors to visit and a concert by a brass band, and before long he was back in Grass Valley for a month-long midsummer reunion with Bertie.

Unremarked in Jim's diary was the February 1898 sinking of the U.S. battleship *Maine* in Havana harbor. In April the U.S. Congress demanded Spain withdraw from Cuba and authorized President McKinley to take retaliatory military action. None of this appears to have seemed very important in distant California until June, when several young men from Grass Valley were called to the colors. On July 14 General Santiago surrendered, and although the Spanish-American War dragged on till December, Grass Valley celebrated this first victory with fireworks.

Back again at Mokelumne Hill, Jim was "very lonesome." The weather was hot, fishing was poor, and he was bored, especially on Saturdays and Sundays. He wrote, "Time is hard to pass," and again, "Do not know what to do to pass the time." On October 13, when weather halted operations in Calaveras County, Jim finally left for Grass Valley. A true Cornishman, Jim always wanted to look his best, and on his way (as he had on each previous trip), he stopped off in Sacramento to buy a new suit.

December 11 was a Sunday. As usual Jim and Bertie went to church, but instead of going for a walk, they both went back to Bertie's house. He must have stayed late. Instead of noting (as he usually did) what time he got home, he wrote, "Birdie, if you should ever read this, you should know the time!"

Christmas Eve was spent with the Peters family, and Jim gave Bertie a pair of gloves, a glove box and perfume. On December 28 he recorded his initiation into the Independent Order of Red Men, a benevolent association of lumbermen. On New Year's Eve he summed up his year:

> 1898 is at an end and we are now to begin another and I hope it will be still better than the last. There was several changes in the last year. On Jan. 16th I turned over a new leaf and tried to be a better boy and I am not sorry I did so and in

this year I also found a girl of my hearts desire and will soon have her for my wife. I left GV three times, once to San Francisco, one to Mokelumne Hill and once to West Point but always glad to return. I also became an Uncle on July 30th by my sister having a young son, Ernest William Rowe.

Some time earlier Jim had taken a correspondence course in electricity. This fitted him for an electrician's job at the North Star Mine's power plant, which would allow him to stay in Grass Valley. Bertie already had persuaded him that she had no intention of living in the wilds of Calaveras County. When Jim had argued that West Point was a healthy place to live, that people lived longer there, Bertie answered, "No—it only seemed longer!" In fact, there is every indication that Jim, too, much preferred living in Grass Valley.

So, with marriage in mind, he decided to build a house. Luckily, the land was available, a present from his father. When

The North Star Mine powerhouse. The stone viaduct beside it carried water over Wolf Creek (foreground) to turn a giant Pelton waterwheel.

they had left West Point, Joel bought two acres of land on Pleasant Street in Grass Valley on which he and Mary built one house and Syndie and her husband built another. Jim planned for a fine two-story house, much more imposing than either of the existing buildings. The lumber came from the mill at West Point, and Jim and his friend James Sampson did all the work themselves. On October 11, 1900, when their new home was finished, James Jenkin Rowe and Alberta Peters were married at Grass Valley.

Alberta's parents, like the Rowes, both came from Cornish mining families. Hugh Peters, Bertie's father, was a timekeeper; he had never worked underground, but due to the nature of mining, he had lived in a number of different places, going wherever work was offered. Clara Mayne, Bertie's mother, was born in Cornwall. Her family had come first to Grass Valley, but they, too, moved frequently, finding work wherever there was hard rock that needed mining. In 1875, while living in Virginia City, 25-year-old Hugh and the beautiful 15-year-old Clara met and were married. By the time Clara was 21 the couple had 5 children, the second of which was Alberta.

Clara Peters was only 40 when her daughter married Jim Rowe. While Hugh Peters was quiet and mild mannered, Clara was loud voiced—a mover and shaker. Winnifred well remembers the times when Hugh would come home and announce that he had been laid off at one or another of the mines. Clara would take off her apron, put on her hat and march out. When she came back, she would tell him, "Hugh, you start at the Empire [or whichever mine was working] on Monday!"

Clara was ambitious for her children and expected them to rise in the world. She took in washing so the girls could go to high school. Both daughters had piano lessons, and when her son went to school in San Francisco she took in a woman boarder. When Clara decided their house was too small for her growing family, more boarders helped pay for a new larger one. And as they grew up, daughters Clarinda and Alberta were expected to help clean house and look after the boarders.

Jim and Alberta settled happily into their new home on

Joel and Mary Jenkin Rowe in front of their house on Pleasant Street in Grass Valley.

Pleasant Street and lived there for the rest of their lives. The house was elegantly furnished. Winnifred Cannon still has the clock, ornate with fretwork, that her parents were given as a wedding present, as well as marble-topped tables from grandmother Peters' house.

The first thing Alberta bought after they were married was the "Cash Buyers' Union" sewing machine she ordered from the Sears Roebuck catalog. It cost $25. Her second purchase was a "Vose" rosewood piano with an ornate piano stool. The hardearned piano lessons had paid off, and Alberta played beautifully.

The couple's first child, Kenneth Theodore Rowe, was born on September 16, 1901. As was customary, the birth took place at home, but a doctor was called in to deliver the baby. Because Alberta was healthy, no one expected the doctor to make a return visit. In 1908 baby girl Winnifred arrived. Ten years later there was a second boy, Delbert, who sadly died of croup in 1920 when he was just 2½ years old.

The three adjacent houses on Neal and Pleasant Streets were built quite close together, and Winnifred and her brother grew up close to their Rowe grandparents. In fact, the proximity of the houses did cause some problems. Jim and Alberta's house was the largest, and the older folks felt he was too extravagant, that the house was too showy for a 25-year-old. Winnifred remembered the house as indeed too big for the lot and their hedge was over the boundary, a fact often pointed out to the young couple.

The house on Pleasant Street was, for the children, a pleasant place to grow up. Jim and Alberta were concerned and loving parents, but very Cornish in that they were quite shy about demonstrating their emotions. This was not a family that hugged and kissed; in fact, the first time Winnifred remembers being kissed was when her parents left her at Berkeley at the start of her freshman year. She remembers, "It was almost embarrassing!"

Social life revolved mainly around family. Friends were welcomed by invitation, but there was no dropping in. The Rowe grandparents still maintained Cornish traditions. Cornish foods, such as steamed suet pudding and clotted cream (known as "scalded cream" in Grass Valley), were made by both grandmothers and by Alberta and Syndie.

Once a week each housewife baked a supply of pasties. A good-sized piece of sirloin steak cost just 25 cents, and the butcher always threw in a piece of kidney suet to be used for the pastry. Pasties, wrapped in layers of newspaper to keep them warm, were a staple in the picnic basket, or served more elegantly for parties at the Masonic Hall. Often there was a pasty in the top compartment of a man's lunch bucket, kept warm by the tea in the bottom section.

If there was dough left over from the pasties, one could make "Eggy 'Obbins." A pasty was shaped and then two raw eggs were slid into the dough casing and baked. In later years Win-

Freeman's Bakery and P. W. Michell's City Market on Main Street.

nifred would make these, and her son Bob so enjoyed them as an after-school snack that her husband Earl Cannon said he never got a chance to taste one until Bob married and left home! Grandma Peters made "heavy cake" and everyone baked bread. However, Winnifred remembers much preferring the Freeman's Bakery bread, which cost ten cents a loaf. She recalls Grandma Peters as the better cook—Grandma Rowe had a tendency to underseason.

True to their Cornish roots, tea was served every day. In Mary Rowe's household the kettle was never off the stove and the teapot would be replenished by simply adding more tea and hot water to the tea leaves in the bottom of the pot, a custom that, in later years, Winnifred protested. On Sunday they drank coffee in the younger Rowes' household, but sometimes Sunday breakfast was typically Cornish, and they would serve dried codfish (nicknamed "Irish Turkey") with English mustard.[2]

Alberta, too, was a good cook, and Winnifred especially remembers her apple pies made with applesauce. In fact, she can never remember a time when there wasn't an apple pie in the pantry. Homemade clotted cream accompanied the pie and was served for breakfast on toast and jam. When Aunt Syndie made saffron buns, their scent pervaded the neighborhood, and eaten warm they were heavenly!

Clara Peters was vain of her own good looks. Winnifred remembers that when someone mentioned Alberta's beauty, her grandmother sniffed, "My daughter isn't as good-looking as I am, and her daughter isn't as good-looking as she is!" Although Hugh had blue eyes, Alberta had brown eyes like her mother. Clara was somewhat ruffled by baby Winnifred's blue eyes; she called her granddaughter "the neighbor's kid"! The neighbors with the blue-eyed children were an Irish family, and Clara Peters had no time for those whom she dubbed "shanty Irish." She didn't think much of her own Cornish folk either. She called them "ignorant Cousin Jacks"!

During the years prior to World War I, Jim continued to work at the power plant. Winnifred remembers the pink moss rose that grew outside the powerhouse door. Her father would pick the flowers and bring them back in his lunch basket. Winnifred remembers her father as the one who looked after any childhood ailments. Sometimes advice was sought from the family doctor, but mostly home remedies were adequate. If either child had a cold, father would set up a hot mustard footbath, chests were rubbed with a mixture of "sweet oil" and turpentine, and there would be hot lemonade at bedtime.

Grass Valley was a great place for families with children. Winnifred especially remembers the annual Sunday School picnics. These were truly the highlights of the year; far more important even than Christmas. On the day before the picnic, families got their tickets for the narrow gauge railroad. That night children got little sleep, and early the next day picnic baskets were packed with pasties, relishes, and a package of tea. Winnifred would be given 25 cents to buy a "goldenrod cake." She still remembers the delicious icing: vanilla on one side, chocolate on the other.

Dressed in their summer best (no jeans in those days!) the

families walked to the Grass Valley depot, where they boarded flat cars—roofed vehicles with open sides and equipped with benches. Everyone hoped to be lucky and get on the same train as the brass band that played all way to their destination near Chicago Park. Once at the picnic grounds, each family settled into a chosen spot and fathers and uncles made little fires to heat the tea kettles. The children played games for prizes donated by Grass Valley businesses, and older children could hike over to Shebley's Pond, where there were waterlilies and boats could be rented. Concessions sold small toys and five-cent ice cream cones; Winnifred always bought a rubber-ball on a big elastic. At five o'clock the whistle blew and everyone headed back to the train.

The Fourth of July was marked by a big parade, and afterwards, as a special treat, there was homemade ice cream, frozen with ice from the Boston Ravine ice house. Chautauqua also made a welcome addition to life in the little town. Every year a big tent was set up and there were plays and concerts. Early in

An Independence Day parade sometime after 1901, when tracks and overhead wires for the electric trolley were placed on Mill Street.

December another parade marked Donation Day. (See Chapters 4 and 7 for more about these processions.)

Christmas was heralded by the Grass Valley Carol Choir. Winnifred remembers the concerts ended with everyone joining in "While Shepherds Watched," sung to the tune of "Diadem." Everyone knew the words and they raised the roof.

Just before the holiday a man came to the house with live turkeys. Unlike today's white turkeys, these had brown feathers. Jim would select one and it would be kept in the yard until he was ready to behead it. In the kitchen a big washtub was filled with boiling water. The turkey's feet were chopped off, and then the bird was dumped on the floor. Everyone had to get down on hands and knees to pluck the feathers. The final chore was to remove the pin feathers; this was done in the kitchen sink and was a fiddly business with tweezers.

About the same time, the Christmas tree was cut and brought into the house. Alberta would hang white linen handkerchiefs round the tree; they looked just like white birds. When visitors came, a handkerchief was taken off and given as a gift. The tree was further decorated with German glass ornaments and red-berried Toyon branches were hung over the pictures. Winnifred did not expect a visit from Santa, because her brother (seven years her senior) had taken pleasure informing her that the old man was a myth. Nevertheless, everyone had at least one or two presents—one was probably something "useful."

Christmas dinner, along with the turkey, stuffing and cranberry sauce, always included cauliflower with cheese sauce, and Winnifred remembers her mother would walk all over town to find cauliflower. Winnifred couldn't remember whether Alberta made Christmas pudding, but Grandma Rowe certainly did.

Revivals were not only religious events but also big social occasions that provided a welcome break to the rather too even tenor of Grass Valley life. Usually the evangelist, plus a trio of musicians and a soloist, came for a week and there were programs each night and every day. The Rowes were conservative in religion as in life, but did go to the revival services. Winnifred remembers the evangelist's powerful voice and Mr. Bennet, the lay leader who cried when full of emotion. In the "Amen Corner" men gave powerful affirmation of their faith. Winnifred remembers one man who got saved every year, and another lady, very Cornish, who wore a hat with feathers that she pulled out, one by one, when in the throes of religious emotion.

In 1917 Jim was offered the opportunity to greatly improve his earnings. The United States had entered the first World War, and an important position at the Empire Mine's cyanide plant was vacant because the incumbent had been called up for military service. Jim took his place, but when the war ended in the following year the soldier returned and got his old job back. Jim then decided to go into the grocery business, although his relatives were not supportive. They warned him he was risking his savings and would find it hard to manage without his monthly paycheck. In fact, some of these same relatives would not trade at Jim Rowe's Grocery Store, and were jealous when it became a success.

Because there were other food stores in Grass Valley, Jim decided to specialize in "Choice and Fancy" groceries. However, true to his Methodist roots, he refused to stock tobacco or alcohol. Winnifred recalls that sugar and flour were bought in 100-pound sacks and then divided into 5-pound bags, and that the store carried many delicacies not common in Nevada County, such as canned crab. The Namco and Geisha brands had big solid pieces of crab meat, rather than the usual shreds, and crab salad became a Rowe family Sunday night tradition. Rowe's store had "charge and delivery" and earned a reputation for good service. It remained in operation until about 1943.

Winnifred well remembers some of Grass Valley's leading citizens and their large houses. The Angove house boasted a fountain in the front yard, along with a life-size statue of an elk. Charles E. Clinch owned the store where miners had to go to get their pay checks. Mrs. Clinch, an impressive erect figure, always wore a white blouse, wide leather belt and black ankle-length skirt. Round her neck she wore a black velvet ribbon. It is said that once someone told the merchant's wife she had a run

Clinch & Company's store on Mill Street.

in her stocking and she responded, "When you're Mrs. Clinch and everyone *knows* you're Mrs. Clinch, you don't have to worry about those things!"

Education was valued in the Rowe household. Even though he never went beyond the eighth grade in school, Jim was a great reader and continued to learn all his life. Jim prided himself on his beautiful handwriting and in his youth had developed quite a thriving business engrossing visiting cards. Winnifred has kept some of these which are quite different from today's plain pasteboards. Instead they are fanciful little works of art, ornamented with pastel flowers and with the names handwritten in fine cursive.

Alberta encouraged her children's studies; Winnifred never remembers being called to do household chores if she was busy reading or studying. In 1925, when she was 16, Winnifred graduated from Grass Valley High School and went off to the University of California at Berkeley. A photo shows a slim sweet-faced girl. But Clara Peters, who never appreciated her granddaughter's looks, sniffed, "A plain face is more protection than a policeman!"

Both Joel Rowe and Hugh Peters died in 1922. In 1932 Alberta's mother died, and Mary Rowe's life ended in 1933. In 1925 Kenneth Rowe was married to Constance Bree, whose father was from Cornwall, and Winnifred married Earl Cannon in 1930. As the children grew more independent, Jim and Alberta grew more and more involved in the Masonic movement. He became "head man" of Madison Lodge, the Royal Arch, and the Knights Templar, and twice was Patron of Eastern Star. Alberta was active in Eastern Star and eventually became Matron. Both were sponsors of Job's Daughters. The Masonic Hall was the center of their social life, and it was where they met their friends.

Jim and Alberta had been married for more than 60 years when Jim died in 1963, followed two years later by Alberta. Their daughter says that she never heard a cross word between them. Winnifred and Earl also had a long happy marriage. When interviewed for this book in 1997, she was a widow living in San Jose, California.

NOTES

1. A donkey engine is a portable steam engine that makes use of revolving drums and cables to haul logs through the woods to a central landing. It was invented in 1882 by John Dolbeer, a partner in the Dolbeer & Carson Lumber Company at Eureka, California. Sometimes donkey engines were mounted on barges to herd floating rafts of logs.

2. Fish, whether codfish, smoked haddock, or kippers was and still is quite a traditional part of a proper English breakfast. Drying was the easiest way to preserve many kinds of fish. Minnie Chinn remembered her mother drying pilchards on the clothesline, and the Chinn family ate "dried codfish, salted salmon bellies, or bloaters" for Sunday breakfast (page 86). In the 1930s the author remembers the roofs of houses in St. Ives, Cornwall, decorated with fish set out to dry. In a letter to the publisher, Mrs. Beverly Rowe Hailer, a Cornish descendant, recalls: "A Sunday breakfast at our home while growing up was creamed codfish; the codfish had to be soaked the night before and the next morning a cream sauce was made and it was served with boiled potatoes."

Chapter 9
The Tremewan Family

The photograph taken in 1902 is proof positive that Frederick William Tremewan had done well in South Africa. Twenty-two-year-old "Bill" is handsome and self-assured in his well-tailored double-breasted tropical suit, and the broad-brimmed hat he carries was surely worn with a flair. This young man had already moved a long way from his birthplace and hometown of St. Agnes, Cornwall and he intended to go even further. But that is in the family tradition.

Bill's father, William John Tremewan, like so many other Cornish, had sought his fortune in the South African mines, was successful, and returned to St. Agnes a fairly wealthy man. He had invested his money in a terrace of houses known as "Glanville Terrace," and in farms, a haulage business and other property. William Tremewan was respected in St. Agnes and served on the local board of education.

He was also Collector of Customs, and his heavy wagon, drawn by great cart horses, was in evidence down at the beach whenever there was a wreck. In view of Cornish skill at avoiding customs duties, one must hazard a guess that the collector's pickings were slim! However, family members remember the time a French ship carrying wine went aground, and William was able to haul away four big barrels.

William had married Harriet Gill and they had eight children, including twins Frederick William and Archibald. William and Harriet's photo depicts a good-looking, well-dressed couple; their children shared their looks.

After his return from South Africa, young Bill did not stay long in Cornwall. There was a family decision that he and Archibald and their older sisters—Dora, Mildred and Ethel—would leave Cornwall for the United States. Their Uncle John Tremewan, William's oldest brother, was already in Grass Valley, and it is probable the Tremewans had friends or even relatives working in Ely, Minnesota. Bill and Archie sailed on

February 7, 1901. On arriving in New York they, like so many of their countrymen before them, stayed at the "Cornish Arms Hotel." Both brothers kept diaries and we know they both went straight to Ely, although Archie only stayed a short time. By July 4 he was at Butte City, Montana, and reached Grass Valley by September.

The diaries of both young men chronicle their daily lives as well as including news from "back 'ome" in St. Agnes. Archie Tremewan wrote, "January 25, 1901: Left St. Agnes." A few days later Bill's diary noted:

Fred William Tremewan in 1902.

> Feb. 7, 1901 Archie and I arrived in Ely Feb 7, 1901, and started to work in Zenith Mine on 11 of Feb. We left home with W. Garveth; J. Gribben; Andrew & Albert Vivian; T. Annear; W. Cowling and W. Gates.

Archie recorded that he, too, went to work in the Zenith. Bill was probably anxious to get back to his own trade of blacksmithing. At the end of the year he wrote:

> Dec. 31, 1901 I went to work at the Pioneer Blacksmith shop, Ely, Minnesota.
> Jan 3, 1902 Grandfather Gill died of congested appleplexy [sic]

and was buried Saturday 20 at the age of 79 years.

Jan 13 Accepted written invitation for an evening party.

It is possible the death of their grandfather changed the family's plans, because here there is a gap in the diary. Bill apparently went back to Cornwall for a short time and returned in June. His next entries note:

June 11, 1902 Arrived Ely.
Aug. 9 Edward VII crowned
Nov. 7 Sister Ethel left home.
Nov. 19 Ethel arrived in Ely.

The diary records the deaths of many friends, both in Cornwall and in the U.S.; many are young miners. Bill himself narrowly avoided tragedy in Ely. When an older miner tells him he has heard the "Tommyknockers" about during his shift underground, Bill is sceptical; he doesn't believe in such superstitions and is not going to miss his day's work.[1] The older man is adamant and threatened to knock Bill down if that is what it would take to keep him home. Bill acquiesced. That day there was a cave-in at the mine.

Sister Ethel arrived in Ely, Minnesota, in November, and then she and Bill left for Grass Valley, arriving on December 11, 1902. There is no mention of the other sisters; perhaps they traveled directly to Grass Valley. Iron mining must have been in one of its periodic depressions. Bill's diary notes that many left Ely to go back to Cornwall, or for California, South Africa or Canada.

During the next years the diary is mostly filled with the comings and goings of Grass Valley friends; however, on January 17, 1908, the news is about a significant victory for the miners, who had been on a long strike to improve their hard lives by adopting the 8-hour work day. Bill wrote: "Strike ended. Miners getting 8 hours."

The year 1908 was a busy one for the Tremewan twins. A carefully preserved newspaper-clipping records: "Quietly wedded in early evening, Miss Inez Sincock, the happy bride of William Tremewan." The writer described a "very pretty wedding" at the bride's home. Both Inez's parents were from Redruth, and her father was a miner. On May 6 of the same year Archie Tremewan married Flora Mills Harris of Grass Valley. Her family was Cornish-born.

1909 was equally momentous. Archie and Flora's son Cecil was born on January 26, the same day sister Winifred, who had remained in Cornwall, married Henry Walters. On June 20 Bill recorded: "Our baby boy born." The baby was named William. On July 7 Archie and Flora sailed for England on the White Star liner *Teutonic*. They stayed in St. Agnes until December 7, when they returned on the *Oceanic*. Archie's diary records: "Had a choppy passage, was not sick all the way coming out nor going home." The couple arrived back in Grass Valley in time for Christmas.

In August 1910 both brothers wrote about a trip to Alberta, Canada, "to look over the country for homestead land." However, the trip was unproductive and the Tremewans both came back to Grass Valley.

During the following years, both Tremewan families grew. Bill and Inez had six children: five boys, William, John, Cecil, Herbert (who died in infancy) and Henry (who died at birth), and a daughter, Betty. Cecil today is custodian of Bill's diary. Archie and Flora had four sons, one of whom also was named Cecil; the other boys were Lawrence, Stanley and Ralph. Ralph has Archie's diary and he, together with his cousin Cecil, was instrumental in putting together the Tremewan family story.

Cecil described his father as a proud, stubborn and opinionated man, but Bill was also a very devoted father. His diary records the birth of each child, and every winter Bill measured and weighed his children and carefully recorded their growth in his diary. The record began at Christmas 1913 when baby Cecil was only 9 months old, and continued without a break until 1930, when 19-year-old son John had already left home—and even though he could no longer measure and weigh all his children, Bill did record John's height. Later, he took equal pains to measure and weigh his grandchildren.

In 1919 Inez's mother, Jennie Sincock, sold them her home, which is still standing on Oak Street in Grass Valley. It was a typical Cornish miner's cottage, although it had been spruced up with Victorian gingerbread, a white picket fence and a front porch. There were two bedrooms, a bath, kitchen and parlor.

That was the year Cecil started school. He well remembered September 16, 1919:

> I was five years old and when my two older brothers started off to school, I had no one to play with, so I went too. Mother offered to take me home, but the teacher said I was happy there and my mother should let me stay. So I started First Grade.

Inez Tremewan died in 1920. A newspaper clipping tucked into Bill's diary is headlined: "Mother of Four Small Children Passes from Life." She was 33 years old and had given birth to daughter Betty just a few weeks earlier. The article stated that her death was due to "the complications of childbirth." For Bill, there was no thought of remarriage. Inez's mother took care of baby Betty, but Bill insisted that "the boys are staying with me." When asked if a housekeeper had been hired, Cecil laughed, saying, "Every time Dad brought in a housekeeper, we boys ran her off!"

Cecil remembered the good food his father cooked. Cornish pasties once a week, saffron buns and seedy cake, meat, potatoes and carrots. All good food Bill had learned to enjoy at his mother's table back in St. Agnes.

The diary and Cecil's memories continued to tell the family story. In 1922 Bill bought a second-hand car, a Durant. This must have been an enormous timesaver, since it was quite a long walk to and from work. As Cecil's wife Barbara remembered, "not many had new cars, and if they did they were immediately scrutinized: 'Where did the money come from?' Jealous neighbors would always suspect highgrading."

This certainly was a possibility. Cecil remembered a good friend, a skinny little boy whose father worked in the Peabody Mine. Near their property was an air shaft, and at regular intervals the lad would be lowered down the shaft to retrieve a tobacco tin containing ore that his father had stashed away. The family did quite nicely!

Apart from a little highgrading, Cecil Tremewan remembers the Grass Valley of his childhood as being a very law-abiding town. Until 1930 the entire police force consisted of two men. One worked day-shift while the other worked night-shift, and they were paid $100 a month, with no time off. To supplement the police, California and other Western States allowed the county sheriff to deputize anyone he needed if an emergency arose. It was considered an honor to be a member of the fire department, and Grass Valley had four fire companies, each with 25 members and 25 auxiliary members who could be called in case of need. In a town where most buildings were made of wood, fire was an ever-present hazard. If there was a big fire, any citizen could be deputized by the firemen, who went down the street, knocked on doors, and told male residents, "You're a firefighter." Cecil Tremewan was deputized more than once, and remembers how the long hose had to be dragged by hand to the site of the conflagration.

The Fireman's Ball was the big social event of the year for which the whole town turned out. The firemen wore their dress uniforms, and the ball started with a memorial to deceased comrades and a Grand March.

Another annual highlight was the Cornish wrestling on the Fourth of July. A ring was set up downtown at the corner of Main and Mill streets, and quite large sums of money were wagered by placing bets on top of an upturned whisky barrel. The wrestlers were of Cornish ancestry, but all from the U.S., and each mine had its champions. Cornish wrestlers wear special canvas jackets and it is considered a foul to touch the opponent's body; instead the straps on the jacket are grabbed, in order to bring the adversary down.

Bill Tremewan never became a U.S. citizen and always kept in close touch with activities in Cornwall and in the rest of England. His diary noted the coronations of Edward VII and George VI, the election of 1910 (in which the Liberal Party was again elected), and the First Prize won by the St. Agnes Choir. Cecil believed that his father always wanted to go back and live in Cornwall, but was afraid that, without property or a job, he might not be able to survive.

Because he was not a citizen, Bill could not vote. However, his sympathies were always with the working man, and he always said he was a Democrat. He was a staunch member of the Mineworkers' Protective League, and while working at the Idaho Maryland Mine he stood up at a meeting and suggested the League work to raise wages to $5 a day. Three days later he got his walking papers and from that moment was "blackballed" from the mine. After that he worked as a blacksmith at other mines, including the Golden Center, which closed in 1926. Later he joined his son William as a blacksmith for the Sierra Railroad. He also became an avid gardener, and in the back of his diary he transcribed the well-known poem, "A garden is a lovesome thing, God wot!"

Music was the joy of Bill's life. He played the violin and belonged to the famous Grass Valley Carol Choir. The singers were all male; the only woman member, Mrs. Polkinghorne, coached the boy altos. Cecil and the other boys sang next to their fathers to learn the words to the hymns and carols. Cecil brought out two pictures of the choir, dated 1903. The men and boys are wearing their best blue serge suits and the men wear bowler ("derby") hats. Among them is Will Trathen, Loretta Henwood's future husband, then a boy of 11 or 12. He must have been growing fast, for his pants are a little short and he is wearing high-topped boots. In the background of the photo is the Royal Shoe Store, and W. D. Harris' undertaking parlor. (The buildings they occupied are still standing.)

Another photograph showed the choir in 1907, standing on the steps of the unfinished State Capitol in Sacramento. The brightly polished boots and shoes indicate the extreme pride of these Cornish miners. A 1909 photo showed Harold Jewell George, 21 years old and very good-looking. He is holding his cornet case (the cornet gave the choir the pitch).

Bill Tremewan never missed a choir meeting, a fact that might have contributed to his death. He was already a sick man at the time, but refused to see a doctor and was determined to

The Grass Valley Carol Choir decked out in their finery.

Singing Cornish carols underground in the Idaho Maryland Mine in 1940. Left to right: Aldo Aranson, Harold Hanson, Oakley Johns, "Scotty" Partington, (unknown man), Bill Bartle, Bill Tremewan, (three unknown men), and Ed Burtner.

go to choir practice. His son and John's father-in-law tried to persuade him that he really belonged in hospital, but, always stubborn, he refused to go. Mr. Thomas called the sheriff, who carted off the reluctant invalid. Sadly, medical help came too late. Frederick William Tremewan died on May 20, 1958. The back pages of his diary testified to his network of friends with addresses in all the mining regions of the U.S., as well as in Canada, Rhodesia and, of course, Cornwall.

Archie's life ran less smoothly. He and Flora divorced when his children were still young, and from then on they saw little of their father. He died in Grass Valley on November 3, 1954. His son Ralph continued to live in Grass Valley, and so was able to share Archie's diary with the author. Archie and Bill's sisters all eventually moved away from Grass Valley: Mildred Blake to Sacramento and Dora Stautenberg to the state of Washington; Ethel Smith went first to Sacramento and then to Aromas, California.

After a 15-month stint working in the Prescott Hill Mine, Cecil Tremewan (Bill's son) left Grass Valley in 1939 to attend college. He knew that if he did not get an education he would be doomed to work as a miner for the rest of his life, and the prospect was not appealing. Business administration seemed a career goal with a more viable future. In Sacramento he met Barbara Ellis on a blind date, and in 1941 they were married. The couple first lived with Barbara's family in Humboldt, California, where Cecil worked as a lumberman, but at the outbreak of World War II they moved to Alameda, where the shipyards were feverishly turning out cargo vessels. Because Cecil's job was important to the war effort, he was exempted from the draft.

Cecil and Barbara continued to live in the San Francisco Bay Area until 1964, when they returned to Grass Valley and bought a men's shop on Mill Street, which they ran until Cecil retired. In 1970 he was able to renew his Cornish roots when he and his wife visited his father's old home in St. Agnes. They stayed with Betty Tredinick, whose father was a first cousin of Cecil's father. Cecil said 1970 marked the 125th anniversary of the St. Agnes Sunday School, and his cousin, along with most other good Methodists in town, went to church every night.

As in the case of so many Cornish Americans, family ties have remained strong. Cecil was happy to share a family tree that showed all the descendants of William Tremewan and Harriet Gill down to the third and fourth generations.

NOTES

1. Tommyknockers, called simply "knackers" in Cornwall, were underground spirits of the mines. A. K. Hamilton Jenkin (in *Cornwall and Its People*) describes them as "small, wizened creatures ... their presence was not considered altogether unlucky, since they were scarcely ever heard or seen except in the neighbourhood of rich lodes."

Chapter 10
Mary Anne Kent

Mary Anne Kent's life history is especially interesting, both because her experiences are so characteristic of those of her contemporaries who emigrated at the turn of the century, and because she is one of only two interviewed by the author from the "first generation."

Mary was born in 1881 in Beacon, Cornwall, near Camborne, and was christened Mary Anne Mitchell. She was the oldest child of William John and Betsie Simmons Mitchell. Her father was a miner and her mother was a farmer's daughter. Mary was still a baby when a sister was born, and another sister and two brothers followed in rapid succession.

The family of seven lived in a small two-bedroom cottage rented from a blind man. Mrs. Kent remembered the brick floor in the kitchen and the linoleum in the front room. There was a cookstove in the kitchen which burned coal; as far as Mary remembered, peat was not used. There were two fireplaces: the living room fire warmed the house in winter, but the bedroom fire was never lit. Though the house did have piped-in water, there was no bathroom. In the kitchen, a tin boiler over its own fire heated the water, and the family bathed in a big tub set up in front of the kitchen stove. Mary remembered the good feeling of the fire-warmed towels. The little house was lighted by kerosene lamps and candles.

Mary said, "I guess everyone had plenty to eat." The family maintained a small garden where they kept chickens: Rhode Island Reds and Plymouth Rocks. They grew their own potatoes, carrots, parsnips, and cabbages. Breakfast was toast and boiled eggs. Lunch might be a little fried ham, or more rarely bacon, with potatoes and cabbage. A piece of cake and a cup of tea in the afternoon was followed by a substantial evening meal of stew or "pasty," the typical Cornish meat turnover. Mary remembered chicken pie as a treat, and she never tasted fried chicken until she came to the United States. Cornish pasties were made regularly, both for the family dinner and for her father's lunch at the mine, and Mrs. Kent was firm about the ingredients of a good pasty: beef, potatoes and turnip. "You could use onion for those as likes onion; I like turnip myself."

To add variety to the meals, Mary's father used to go down to St. Ives to buy fish straight off the fishing boats: "Mackerel, whiting, herring, ling, congers [eel], hake and cod. Father liked salmon, too—but that was canned. There was always plenty of both whole and skim milk, as well as butter and cream."

When Mary was seven she started school. Her first school was in a little house. Public education had become the law in 1870, but 15 years later was not yet implemented in remote Cornwall. For this early education the Mitchell family paid a penny a week to Mrs. Honey, the teacher. The first day of school, Mrs. Kent remembered wearing a pinafore and lace-up boots. Her hair was neatly braided.

The following year the first village school was opened, and every day, rain or shine, Mary would walk to school. She remembered they did not have raincoats then, only coats, and it did rain often in Cornwall. The two teachers, Miss Stevens and Miss Brooks, presided over a big multigrade classroom. The boys and girls sat separately and the seats were "joined together, all in a row."

Mary was still quite small when her mother died. Left with five young children, her father must have felt fortunate to have soon found a second wife, but his eldest daughter appears to have had some problems with her new stepmother. Mary recalled how hard the work at home was. On washdays it was her job to scrub the smaller items, such as handkerchiefs and the detached collars for her father's and brothers' shirts. Ironing was with flat irons put to heat in the stove. When they were properly hot it was necessary to fish them out with a poker and put them in a metal "box" in order to iron the clothes. The girls' school pinafores were sent out to the laundry to be "mangled" at a charge of a penny or so for several pieces.

Mary clearly remembered the Condurrow Mine where her father worked. She used to take him his dinner, always a pasty well-wrapped to keep it warm. She had to pass the sheds where the women bal maidens worked. The first time she noticed a big wheelbarrow, she remarked to one of the men that it was "a funny wheelbarrow with no wheels." He showed her that it was, in fact, a big metal bin full of ore and that the two women walking, one each side, were carrying it by straps around their necks.

After Condurrow Mine closed the only work available was at Dolcoath, known as the deepest and most dangerous mine in Cornwall. "Deep as Dolcoath" was a well-known local saying. Mary's father decided to join other Cornish in the mines of South Africa. His friends begged him not to go because so many never returned from abroad, but he answered: "I would rather go to Africa and die of fever than go to Dolcoath and be killed." Shortly after he reached South Africa William Mitchell did indeed die of typhoid fever.

In those years the Methodist Church and its tenets structured the Mitchells' family life. Mary remembered that on Saturday all the vegetables needed for the Sunday dinner would be cleaned and all the water drawn. The children had "everyday clothes" (which were worn to school), "holiday clothes" (for Saturdays and school vacations), and "Sunday clothes." Sunday shoes had to be brushed on Saturday: "If we wore our Sunday shoes on Saturday and dirtied them, we could not brush them on Sunday." On Sunday morning each child's best clothes were laid out on the bed. The whole family went to Church and Sunday School. There was an annual Sunday School picnic, and once a year the choir all piled into one big carriage for an all-day outing to either Penzance or Falmouth.

When Mary was 12 she left school. Many of her friends went to work at that age as domestic servants or in the gunpowder factory where blasting powder was manufactured, but Mary's stepmother kept her home to help with the younger children. At 13 Mary got a position as child's maid for a woman she described as "a relative of Queen Victoria."

She recalled: "I had had experience looking after my brothers and sisters at home, so this lady, who was a relative of Queen

Victoria, gave me a position as child's maid." Mary's mistress was a young woman whose name was Mrs. Jenniver, and her husband had been employed by her family as a tutor. The runaway marriage of teacher and young pupil must have caused a scandal. "Her folks never forgave her," Mary remembered.

> Her mother did come to Cornwall to visit, she was an older woman and she dressed like the old Queen, all in black, but the father never came to the house and Mrs. Jenniver never visited her family.

The young mother was, according to Mary, not very good-looking. Mary remembered: "She had a dark complexion and was very plainly dressed. But they were very good Church of England people and she was a beautiful piano player." The husband had founded a boys' school, the Clemens School, and taught boys from the wealthier local families. Mary remembered "two young gentlemen from Hayle: Oscar Trevithick and a member of the Polkinghorne family." Sadly, Mrs. Jenniver's baby died of pneumonia at the age of 9 months, and the young nursemaid returned home.

Mrs. Kent's daughter, Gladys Bray Clemo, told the author that during the next few years Mary lived at home and helped her stepmother with the care of the growing Mitchell family.

On Christmas Eve 1900 Mary Anne Mitchell was married to William Prisk Bray at the Redruth Registry Office. The young bride, not quite 20, wore a long-skirted gray dress and a matching hat. Her husband, who was just her own age, was a miner.

The new century marked the end of an era, both for England and for Mary. On January 22, 1901, she heard the church bells toll for the death of Queen Victoria. During the next two years, Gladys and William John were born in Mary's own bedroom in the Bray's little cottage at Brae Por. Mary's stepmother was the midwife and Mary was kept in bed for two weeks.

William Bray had gone to work in "deep Dolcoath," the mine Mary's father had so feared. Mary was not happy about this, but it was the only mine offering work and William had to support his young family. The baby, William John, was only a year old and his sister Gladys still under four when William Bray was killed in a cave-in. At 25 Mary was a widow. The mine offered aid, but true to her Cornish heritage of sturdy independence, Mary turned it down; she did not want to be beholden to anyone. To support her children she took in boarders, cooking and cleaning for two or three young miners. She also did housework, taking the two children with her.

It was at her stepmother's house the following Christmas that Mary met Nicholas Thomas Kent, whose brother had recently married Mary's sister. Nick had been left a widower two weeks before Mary's own bereavement, but he had no children. Mary learned that he had been born in Portreath, where he worked on the dock discharging the coal off the colliers. The coal was used to power the steam engines in the mines. Nick and his brother had decided to seek their fortunes abroad, and shortly after this meeting both men left for America. Mary's sister soon followed her husband.

During the next two years letters from Nick Kent punctuated the even tenor of Mary's life. In 1907 he wrote to ask if Mary would join him in Arizona and become his wife; he promised to be a good husband and a good father to her children. Mary said later, "I thought about it, and I prayed about it." In the end she decided: "In America my children would have a good education and a good living, and I thought it my duty to come."

The preparations had to be made rather rapidly. In the summer of 1907 her fiance had written to her that his younger brother would be leaving for the States in September. Nick thought it would be good if she had some help on the trip, especially since her children were still quite young: William was three, and Gladys not quite six years old.

Preparations for the journey were time consuming, but Mary's family gave her a great deal of help. Her sister and her sister's husband were in Arizona already, so the relatives were well aware of the proper way to pack for the voyage. All the family's household goods, including bedding, had to go into one big packing case. Mary brought her own sewing machine and her silver cutlery, including fish knives! The relatives helped Mary cord up the boxes and warned her that she should be prepared to untie the them herself in New York, where the customs officials were known to be "difficult."

The family left the port of Southampton on September 14, 1907. They traveled with 13 men, women and children, all from Cornwall and all from mining families. This was, she told me, an unusually large party to be emigrating together. One young couple was newly married. There were two young men, one of whom was Nick Kent's brother.

In New York it was raining, but Mary heeded her relatives' advice and untied all her own boxes and bags. The customs man hardly checked her baggage, but the newlywed couple had all their goods turned out on the ground. After a man had been paid to retie the boxes, the Bray family and young Kent boarded the train for the four or five days journey to Globe, Arizona, where Nick Kent was working in the copper mines. Here there was a joyful reunion with Mary's future husband, Nick Kent, and her sister and her sister's husband, who was Nick's brother. It took a couple of days for the baggage to arrive, and then, in the brand new home Nick had prepared for his family, Mary Ann Bray and Nicholas Thomas Kent were married. The bride wore a cream-colored dress, and the September day was warm and sunny. Mary told her daughter Gladys that after they were married the people in Globe had a "chivaree." According to custom, the children crashed cans together and made a noise until paid off with nickels or dimes. Things may have got a little out of hand when a rock was rolled down the hill—and went straight through someone's window!

The Kent family lived in Globe for just over two years, and two daughters were born here, Myrtle in 1908 and Elsie in 1910. Elsie was still under a year old when Nick heard of a better opportunity in Sonora, Mexico. Mary Anne bravely packed up and, taking her four children, accompanied her husband south of the border. Mary remembered the soft calls of the Mexican wood gatherers and said she picked up a few Spanish phrases. In Sonora there were other Cornish families and Gladys Bray Clemo remembers going to a private school with an American teacher, Miss Doxler, who came from Los Angeles; the children rode a trolley down to the smelter.

The Kent family stayed in Mexico only nine months. Mary's brother, Arthur Mitchell, had immigrated to Grass Valley and Nick's brother and Mary's sister had recently joined him there. Mary and Nick decided to take their young family and try their luck in the gold mines. Their decision raised eyebrows among their friends in Arizona, who wrote: "Why would you want to go to California? There's nothing but a bunch of English there, you'll never find a job." But, nevertheless, they made the journey.

The Kents arrived in Grass Valley in 1910. At first, they stayed with Mary's sister. Later they moved into a house on South Auburn Street. The young woman loved the town from the moment she first saw the place. Mary said, "It was so pretty!" Not the least of her joys was to find that the "bunch of English" were in fact fellow Cornish. When her sister said to her, "We're going down to see a Cousin Jennie," Mary replied, "We don't have any cousins named Jennie." She had never hear the Cornish called Cousin Jacks and Cousin Jennies until she came to California.

Quite a few other things surprised Mary when she first came to Grass Valley. For one thing, she had never seen a screen door before. She was delighted, though, to find that English foods such as kippers and codfish were available, and she remembered that a friend used to bring clotted cream (called "scalded cream" in Grass Valley) every week. She also remembered seeing a motorcar for the first time; the "Tin Lizzie" was the proud possession of a friend on Whiting Street.

As soon as they arrived, the family joined the Grass Valley Methodist Church, and this too produced some surprises. In the U.S. people talked in church and visitors were introduced: "Imagine me speaking out in church!" Such goings-on would not have been considered "fitty" in Cornwall, but none the less Mary was impressed by the friendly informality of her new neighbors.

During the next years, through World War I, Mary stayed home with her young children and Nick worked in the Empire

Mine along with Mary's brother and brother-in-law. In 1919 her 17-year-old daughter Gladys was married to Cornishman Fred Clemo. And then in 1921, when she was 40, Mary had another daughter, Fay.

The family's life revolved around the Grass Valley Methodist Church. Nick became a lay preacher and he preached on Sundays at the county hospital. He was head usher at the church, and Fay Kent Dreith reminded her mother how he always sat at the back "and sang so loud that everyone knew he was there." All Mary's daughters sang in the choir, and Mary smiled as she said she was the only one in the family who couldn't sing—and she loved to sing!

The Kents, like the other Cornish, loved picnics. There were frequent church picnics, and on Labor Day the special Miners' Picnic. Every family brought its own food, and there was a lot of beer drinking, which may have disturbed the stricter Methodists. There were also picnics at Shebley's Pond which involved a half hour's trip on the old narrow gauge railroad. The children would play games and compete in egg-and-spoon and sack races and the adults played horseshoes, while the band entertained everyone.

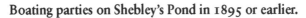

Boating parties on Shebley's Pond in 1895 or earlier.

Young William John Bray and the two oldest girls were all working by 1928, when Nicholas Kent died, but Mary's youngest daughter Fay was only seven. Once again aid was offered, and once again Mary, although no longer young, preferred to rely on her own resources to survive. These were the years of the Great Depression. Mary said, "the depression was not noticeable in Grass Valley, but my son William had a charge account at the restaurant to feed anyone who came through needing a meal."

Mary grew old in Grass Valley. She never returned to the land of her birth. She could have gone back one time, but was taking care of an old lady and felt her duty was to stay. When asked what in Cornwall she remembered with most pleasure, she smiled and said, "The cuckoos that sang in the spring." Without a moment's hesitation she recited the rhyme she had learned in the village school nearly a century before:

> Cuckoo, cuckoo, hello to you!
> In April, he tunes his bill:
> In May, he sings all day:
> In June, he'll change his tune:
> In July, away he'll fly!
> In August, away he must.
> Cuckoo, cuckoo, goodbye to you!

She was still smiling as, once again, she dozed off.[1]

NOTES

1. Mary Ann Mitchell Kent was interviewed in 1979, when she was over 98 years old. Because she died before the planned third interview, there were some gaps in the record of her long and eventful life. In 1994 Mary's daughter, Gladys Bray Clemo, was able to fill in some of these gaps.

Chapter 11
Ed Farley

Emigration from Cornwall to Nevada County lasted from the late 1840s until 1954, finally ceasing when the great Empire Mine closed. Ed Farley was thus a member of one of the last groups of miners to come to Grass Valley. Still hale and hearty in 1979, he was happy to tell his own story, which reiterated the theme of economic distress we have noted in most of the life histories, but also showed the strength of the adventurous and restless spirit of the Cornish even in the 20th century.

Ed Farley was born in St. Just, Cornwall in 1906, the second of five children of Edward Farley and his wife Charlotte. Ed realized early in life that the tin mine dominated the economy of his home town. Whenever the price of tin dropped there was no work, and miners' families were forced onto public relief. This is exactly what happened at the end of World War I. Metals once so vital to the war industries were no longer in demand; the tin market collapsed. Ed's father was unemployed and the whole family had to subsist on the meager 13 shillings a week provided by "the Parish."

To try to make ends meet, Ed's mother walked several miles to St. Buryan to the gardens where flowers were grown for the London market. Here she worked all day as a picker, and then in the evening 12-year-old Ed came with donkey and cart to bring her home. After about three months even the slim relief allowance was cut off, and the mine families were dependent on the Salvation Army soup kitchen. Father Walke, who later gained some national fame as a Cornish eccentric, also set up a soup kitchen to feed the people.

Music was an important part of Ed's life, even as a child. He sang in the choir of the St. Just parish church. He smiled as he remembered "the longest walk of my life."

> One Sunday morning, two or three of us got to talking. Canon Taylor pointed for us to go to the Belfry, to leave the church. Walking down that aisle in front of everyone was the

longest walk of my life. When I went home, I got it from my father, and then on Sunday next, I got it again from Canon Taylor!

When he was 14 Ed got his first job, above ground at Levant Mine. "In those days," he recalled, "the men called us 'pussy cats,' the guys would bring lunches and I'd make tea and heat up their lunches." The pay was about ten shillings a week. Later he got a job chipping rust off an old freighter that was being dismantled for salvage, and then at 17 he went to work underground at Geevor Mine.

By 1928 the young man was doing well enough to buy a motor bike, and he was photographed proudly astride the shiny monster. He remembered paying £7 ($35) for it, and it was the sale of this machine that financed his passage to America.

In 1929 Ed Farley left Cornwall for Flint, Michigan, where he planned to join his older brother, William John Farley, who had emigrated a year earlier. Ed traveled with seven or eight other young men from St. Just, embarking at Liverpool on the *Afghania*, and he remembered how desperately and miserably seasick he was.

Looking down the aisle of the St. Just parish church, where Ed Farley said he took the longest walk of his life.

Once again we notice a familiar theme, the older relative who paved the way. It is also plain that economic motives were not the only source of Ed's decision to leave St. Just. The young man smiling from the seat on the motor bike clearly had places to go, opportunities to seize that were not to be found in the restricted life of West Cornwall. He might have gone to London, but it is doubtful that city life would have appealed to someone of his active temperament. Many young men from St. Just had already gone overseas; Ed decided to follow their example.

When Ed arrived in Flint, he imagined it would easy to get work in one of the auto plants, but in late 1929 "you couldn't buy a job," he said. "Thousands were lined up outside the Buick and Chevrolet factories, and people were eating out of garbage cans."

John Hollow, a friend from St. Just who had come over on the same ship, had intended to stay with an uncle in Detroit, but there was vast unemployment in that city too, so John had gone on to Minnesota, where he found work in the iron mines at Ely. John wrote to Ed, telling about his good fortune, and so Ed arrived in Ely in 40-below-zero weather in February 1930.

Ed Farley well remembered his first shift in the iron mine. His job was to carry timber for the miners, and the work was rugged. He had found lodging with Mr. Pengelly (who had been his Sunday School teacher in St. Just), but Ed was homesick, hated the work and the climate; unfortunately, he was unable to return to England, for he lacked both the money and the will to repeat the misery of his seasick passage.

More serious problems followed: there was a cave-in at the mine and Ed got "blasted." His skull was fractured, and for a time no one knew whether he would live. During his long convalescence the young man, who had always been so strong and independent, was bedridden, totally unable to work, and completely dependent on the kindly Mr. Pengelly. Ed recalled this as a low point in his life, and remembered he was so depressed that he did seriously consider going back to Cornwall.

In 1933 things finally took a turn for the better. John Hollow, Ed's long time buddy, had by this time left Minnesota to join another uncle in Grass Valley, and he wrote Ed, suggesting that he also move out west.

Grass Valley changed Ed's whole attitude about the United States. From the moment he arrived, he knew he would like the place. Although the October 1929 stock market crash had precipitated a severe depression in most of the U.S., Grass Valley and Nevada City were protected enclaves, thanks to the newly reopened mines and President Franklin Roosevelt's decision to raise the price of gold to an unprecedented $35 an ounce in 1933. Ed found immediate work at the booming Pennsylvania Mine.

Perhaps hungry for activity after the long hiatus in Minnesota, Ed plunged into the local social whirl. He arrived on a

The Carol Choir singing underground in 1940. Left to right: M. Henry Argall, Claude Pratt, Harold Hansen, Eldon Hutchinson, "Scotty" Partington, Ed Farley, Bobby George, George Stevens, Harold T. George, Bobby Pyle, Jim Nile, Oakley Johns, Howard Phillips, Mel Hamilton, and Harold J. George (conducting).

Ed Farley operating a hoist in 1939.

Wednesday and on the very next Friday night he was rehearsing with the Methodist Church choir, a group with which he was to sing for over 40 years. Soon his powerful voice was heard with the Grass Valley Octet and the Gold Miners' Chorus, and he was a soloist with the Grass Valley Carol Choir for more than 30 years.

One of Ed Farley's most precious possessions was a recording of the Carol Choir made for the National Folklore Society and the Library of Congress. This choir was first organized in the 1870s, originating with the rather informal groups of miners who gathered together to sing Christmas carols. The eight carols they had recorded were "Seraphic Minstrels," "Lo! The Eastern Sages Rise," "The Lord Is Come," "Bethlehem," "Salutation," "Prince of Life," "Hark What Music," and "Diadem." The style is typically 18th century baroque, and the music is arranged for boy altos, first and second tenors, and basses.

At this point Ed Farley's life history must be linked with that of Minnie Chinn (see Chapter 7). This forceful young lady had told her friends she would *not* marry a miner, she would *not* marry a Cousin Jack, and she would *not* marry anyone younger than herself. She changed her mind, however, when she met Ed Farley at a church choir practice, for he was all three of these.

Minnie already had heard about the new man in town and had bet her girl friends she could get a date with him, but they maintained he was indifferent to Grass Valley girls, and they did not believe she had much chance. It was raining on the night of the choir practice, and at the close Minnie got her umbrella and prepared to walk home. Ed took the umbrella and offered to escort her. It was the beginning of a lifelong romance; Ed Farley and Minnie Chinn were married on October 13, 1934.

Minnie Chinn Farley died in 1996 at the age of 94, having outlived both her husband and her brother Caleb.

Chapter 12
Back 'Ome and Over 'Ere—
Cornish Values

Gwell yu gwytha es gouyn:
It is better to work than to beg
—Old Cornish Saying[1]

John Rowe, himself a Cornishman, has described the Cornish as "Clannish yet individualistic, romantic yet practical and realistic, cautious and reckless." He notes that, in spite of Cornwall's motto, "One and All," quarrels and feuds among family members are not uncommon, and rivalries between towns are the rule.[2]

Cornish miners were known for their technical skills, their independence and initiative, virtues encouraged by the system of tutwork and tribute common in Cornwall until the beginning of the 20th century. The miner was accustomed to assessing his own chances and being responsible for his own mistakes. When events in Cornwall threatened the economic viability of his family, independence and initiative were the very characteristics that made it possible for the miner to seek his fortune overseas.

Because men worked in family teams, it was quite common for them to emigrate together, or at least for the senior member to send for his "pare" as soon as he got established. Because the safety of the team, as well as its profits, had for so long depended on their own judgment and knowledge, these faculties had been well-developed.

On the other hand, used to relying on their own judgment, Cornish miners did not easily take to supervision by others. The story is that when the "company man" came into a level the miners would sit on their shovels until he left. That most of the early captains in Grass Valley were themselves Cornishmen is a tribute not only to their superior knowledge of mining, but also to their understanding of the distinctive breed of miners they supervised.

Cornish "clannishness" is another characteristic frequently mentioned by those who lived and worked with them. It was said that every time a Cornishman got a job, he would ask the mine superintendent, "'ave 'e a job for my Cousin Jack?" So, in the U.S. mining communities, all Cornishmen came to be called Cousin Jacks. The origin of the female equivalent, Cousin Jennie, is obscure. Certainly Jennie is a common name for Cornish or Welsh women, deriving from Jennifer and harking back to King Arthur's Guinevere.

Edmund Kinyon came to Grass Valley before 1914. In October 1950 he recorded his first impressions of the townfolk:

> When the writer came to the Southwest at the beginning of the present century, he first heard the designation "Cousin Jack." It transpired that the mining camps were thronged with workmen so depicted, but full realization of the extent of the migration did not come for another ten years when he came to Grass Valley. . . . It then almost seemed that he had stepped into a foreign country.
>
> Fully three-fourths of the people were of Cornish birth or descent. And that latecomer was amazed at the odd ways of some of them, and the almost unintelligible dialect they spoke.[3]

Cornish names also were strange and often hard to pronounce or, like "Crase" and "Uren," might provoke mirth in America; but the names were good enough "over 'ome" and the Americans would just have to get used to them.

Bob Paine credited the Cornish with "heroic virtues," pointing out that "they brought law and order to the West. And stability. And love of flowers, of home and family life." But he also was aware that not everyone loved the Cornish. In the early days "Cousin Jack" evoked envy, jealousy and even hatred, for it seemed that every position in the mine was reserved for yet another cousin from Cornwall.[4]

As one studies the life histories in this book, the paramount role of religion is immediately apparent. And, to most Cornish, religion meant membership in the Methodist Church. William C. George's diary, together with the Reverend J. H. Maddux's obituary on John George, well illustrates the depth and temper of the religious faith of the Cornish. On board ship the little party had observed the Sabbath even when it was too rough for divine service. In California, as soon as they arrived in Forest City, John and William C. George joined the local Methodist Church, attending services and class meetings.

The peaceful acquiescence surrounding John George's death must be noted. The Cornish miner and his family lived always within the shadow of death, whether from accidents or from lingering lung disease. Perhaps because of this, the relationship of the Cornish to the hereafter was a very special one which is typically illustrated by the hymn verses John recited to the Reverend Maddux, emphasizing eternal rest in the Savior's bleeding side.

Wesleyan hymns proclaimed the theology of the church. It has been said, "Hymns were to the Methodist Church what creeds were to the Established Church."[5] Even the casual reader is aware of the powerful and often bloody imagery of these 19th century hymns. E. P. Thompson has indicated that these hymns, as well as Methodist sermons and tracts, associated joy with sin and guilt, and pain with goodness. Grace is to be found by performing painful, laborious and self-denying tasks.[6] This must have afforded great comfort to the Cornish, for their lives in this world were certainly burdened with such tasks. Life in Cornwall was brutal. The life expectancy of a miner was only 40 years.

As Gage McKinney has pointed out: "Methodism's message of deliverance through faith gave thousands the hope of a better life in another world, if not in this one, as it restored them to a community of believers."[7] John George's ready acceptance of his fate was a product of his lifetime as a faithful follower of the Wesleyan tradition.

The Methodist Church provided spiritual nourishment, but also a way of life for the whole family. "Methodism was an active faith that called for belief in possibilities, and as such it helped men and women gain self-assurance and qualities of character that could enable them to seize their limited opportunities and turn them to account."[8] The norms were honesty, chastity, sobriety and moderation, as well as hard work; sloth was regarded as inconsistent with religion.[9] Patriotism was considered a virtue. In Britain, Methodist preachers had insisted that allegiance to King and Government was a spiritual imperative;[10] in America this allegiance was soon transferred to the government of the United States.

The rules of the church were stringent. Dancing and theatergoing were prohibited, as well as card playing, and of course, drinking. Although a period of "probation" was a prerequisite to full church membership, most probationers did become full members.

Like their counterparts in Cornwall, the first generation of Grass Valley Methodists were strict Sabbatarians. Sunday was a "day of rest" in the most literal sense; no work of any kind was allowed, and since housecleaning, cooking and sewing were women's work, these too were forbidden on the Sabbath. In many families the children could not play with their everyday toys on Sundays, though they might play with cards designed to teach about Biblical figures. On Sunday mornings there were church services; on Sunday afternoons Sunday School, and on Sunday evenings the teenagers attended meetings of the Epworth League, followed by still another church service.

The records of the Grass Valley Methodist Church show how much church activities permeated the everyday lives of the Cornish. In 1873 there were no fewer than 12 Sunday School classes offered. Attendance in each class ranged from 9 to 21 members, and the meetings were held on Wednesday evenings and Saturday afternoons as well as on Sundays. In 1874 there were 231 church members and 350 Sunday School students. By 1876 these numbers had grown to 276 members and 550 in Sunday School, and the subsequent increase was steady.

For many Cornish women the church provided their only social outlet outside the family. The Ladies Aid Society gave women a chance to make and meet friends as they enjoyed refreshments and crafted useful articles for poorer neighbors. In addition, the women hosted the "Old Ladies Tea," an annual church event. In the photograph (see page 53) taken just before

HO! HO!
A DAY IN THE WOODS!

Union ✦ Sunday ✦ School

PICNIC

The Methodist, Congregational and Episcopal Sunday Schools of
Grass Valley will unite in an

EXCURSION AND PICNIC

To Chicago Park

WEDNESDAY, JUNE 8, 1892.

FARE FOR THE ROUND TRIP.

Pupils of these Schools under 18 years, free.   Gentlemen, $1.00,   Ladies, 50 cts
Children, not Members of the Schools, 50 Cents.

Cars for Lunch Baskets will be in readiness at the depot at Grass Valley on Tuesday Evening, June 7.   Baskets should be in by 8 o'clock of that evening.

Trains will leave Depot at 9:25, 11:30 A. M., and 1:20 P. M.
Returning will leave the Grounds at 3:00 and 5:30 P. M.

✦ GAMES. ✦

A variety of games for the entertainment of both old and young, such
as Base Ball, Foot Ball, Grace Hoop, etc., etc. will be furnished

Grass Valley Brass and Reed Band

Under the leadership of Prof. Jenkins is preparing some Excellent
Music for the occasion.

THE PUBLIC ARE CORDIALLY INVITED.

NEEDHAM BROS. PRINT.

World War I, the old ladies look really old—many are wearing
capes and bonnets. Some younger women in long skirts and
shirtwaist blouses smile approvingly in the background.

In the Grass Valley of the 1930s the relationship between the
various churches in town was friendly. The Methodist congregation was the largest. The Salvation Army was second in the
size of its membership. Not all Cornish were Methodists; Grass
Valley's wealthiest church, Emmanuel Episcopal, was organized

in 1855, and had some Cornish members from its inception, including Nicholas and Rebecca Bice. In addition, the Grass Valley Congregational Church, organized in 1853, had a number of Cornish members.

Saint Patrick's Catholic Church served the large population of Irish and Italians who had preceded the Cornish to Grass Valley, and many Germans and Portugese as well. Once a year all the Sunday Schools got together for the big United Sunday School Picnic, each contributing food or drink. The Salvation Army band marched to the picnic ground. Usually the relationship between the Methodists and the Salvation Army was particularly close and friendly. Many of the Methodist men, like George Chinn, played in the Salvation Army band or gave testimony at street corner meetings, as William H. George did.

Salvation Army Brigadiers Howard and Eloise Sloan were stationed in Grass Valley in the 1930s as young Captains. It was their first post, and they remembered clearly the unique relationship they both enjoyed with the Cousin Jacks. They were happy to share memories that shed a good deal of light on the Cornish character.

Back in Cornwall the Salvation Army had appealed to the Cornish partly because of its strong musical tradition. No less than their cousins the Welsh, the Cornish loved music. Great choral singing had been a feature of the Methodist chapels, and John Wesley encouraged his followers to "sing lustily." However, few Cornish would have had the opportunity to study band music were it not for the Salvation Army. Brigadier Sloan pointed out that in England the Army had been classified as a "movement" rather than as a "church," and so it was perfectly acceptable for the Cornish to attend Methodist Chapel on Sunday morning and in the afternoon go out to preach and give testimony and sing and play with the Salvation Army band.

Some American Salvation Army people were a little perturbed by the Cornish insistence on remaining Methodists while coming to Salvation Army meetings, but the Cousin Jacks would explain, "Over 'ome we belong to do it this way." The Sloans were more than willing to let them continue in this fashion at Grass Valley, although this did lead to one slightly embarrassing situation.

One Sunday Howard Sloan came into the meeting and stood at his usual place at the front of the hall. To his surprise, instead of the usual small Sunday choir, the entire choir of the Methodist Church, resplendent in choir robes, marched in. It appeared they had a difference of opinion with their pastor over the question of whose prerogative it was to select the music for the Sunday service. With a fine display of Cornish independence, they simply walked out. For two more Sundays the same thing happened, and then Sloan issued his own ultimatum: the choir was welcome to stay, but the choir robes must be returned. Several members stayed and eventually joined the Salvation Army, but the rest drifted back to the Methodist Church. Sloan smiled as he remarked that the Methodist pastor understood the Cornish and most of the time was able to cope with his independent-minded congregation.

The Sloans had arrived in Grass Valley as newlyweds and moved into a small furnished house provided for their use. Although they were on the slimmest of salaries, nevertheless they wanted to make their first home their own, and after living for a time with the strangely assorted furniture that had come with the house, they decided they should ask for a small loan and go ahead and buy at least bedroom and dining room furniture. Howard Sloan went to his superior officer, who was quite willing to authorize an advance in pay, and the two young people went off to Sears and Roebuck, happy to find that $250 would be ample to furnish bedroom and dining room and could even be stretched to allow for a new rug.

When the new furniture arrived the couple proudly set it in place, relegating to the back room some of the older pieces which had come with the house. They were feeling rather pleased with themselves when their first visitor arrived. She looked around, said nothing, but accepted a cup of tea. Finally, the subject was broached: "Where did 'ee put that chair, the one with the green seat? Mam brought that from back 'ome and it do be a good 'un." The Sloans were a little embarassed as they brought in the missing item. Their visitor finished her tea and stood up to leave. Once again there was silence as she looked straight at Howard. "Now, don't 'ee forget, Cap'un, tes our plaace to take care of the officers!"

The Sloans learned that it was just as well to adapt themselves to the way of life of the Cornish, for the Cornish were not about to adapt their ways to those of America. The officer who had preceded them had allowed his children to go to the movies, and the Cornish demonstrated their disapproval by refusing to put any money in the collection plate when it was passed at the Sunday meeting. This form of sanction was also used if the congregation considered that the officer or his wife were too extravagant. But even when money was withheld, food would be dropped by the house, or the officer and his family would be invited to dinner, for the duty to take care of the officers was taken seriously.

Strict Sabbatarianism was in accordance with the Sloans' own religious beliefs, but they had some lessons to learn from the Cousin Jacks. It was the custom in America for the Salvation Army to sell copies of their newspaper *The War Cry* after the Sunday meeting, but the Cornish would not buy or sell on the Sabbath, so Howard Sloan was obliged to go door-to-door to deliver the paper. At each home he was expected to come in and visit, and since the miners worked three shifts, someone was always having dinner. Howard said he ate so many dinners he gained 40 pounds.

Cornish pride was a characteristic mentioned by Howard and Eloise Sloan. Houses were neat and clean, and in the kitchen the stove gleamed from stove blacking and the stove pipe shone from elbow grease and polish. Equal attention was paid to the Salvation Army meeting hall. If there was a little cobweb in the corner, the Captain would be called aside: "Look 'ee 'ere, Capun, do 'ee see this," and it was expected that the offending cobweb be promptly removed.

The same careful attention was devoted to personal appearance. Work clothes might be well-worn, but they were carefully washed and mended and never ragged. On Sundays the whole family was smartly turned out, the ladies wearing their fanciest hats and the men in their best navy-blue suits.

After just a short while in Grass Valley, Eloise Sloan became pregnant. Since this was their first baby, the couple decided to keep their secret to themselves. However, because she played the piano at the meeting, Mrs. Sloan's thickening figure eventually became evident. One Sunday Katie Chinn called Captain Sloan aside.

"Cap'un Sloan, do 'ee mind my saying something?" she asked. Sloan, not knowing what to expect, assured her she should say what was on her mind.

"Well, see 'tes like this 'ere. When 'ee both came to Grass Valley, Mrs. Sloan looked so pretty up on the piano bench, 'er be so trim. Do 'ee think she be letting 'erself go?"

Howard had no choice but to let Katie in on their secret, whereupon followed a litany of advice. "Now, Capun, do 'ee be careful. Don't let 'er 'ang up clothes. . . . 'tes not fitty for 'er to cross 'er legs." Katie, who had suffered so many problems during her own pregnancy, was concerned, but she was also to be trusted, and she kept the Sloans' secret.

The reference point for all Cornish behavior was "over 'ome." "Over 'ome we always do this" settled any arguments about propriety. Howard Sloan chuckled as he remembered that even the making of Cornish pasties was judged by the over 'ome yardstick. It was traditional for the Salvation Army ladies to make pasties, and the Brigadier recalled a heated argument in the kitchen over whether "proper" pasties should be crimped to the left or to the right!

One of the Cornish customs brought to America involved the financing of the rent for the meeting hall. Years before, a "rent league" had been set up. Those members who could afford it would contribute a small amount each month towards the rent, and it was customary for the officer to visit each household or business to collect the 25 cents or so from each. By Sloan's day this had become a nuisance; the amount was so small it could easily have been budgeted from the general funds. But no matter: "Over 'ome we always do it this way," so the custom was continued.

Another old country (and Methodist) standard, upheld by at least the first generation Cornish, was the abhorrence of card and dice games. This posed a problem for the young Sloans, who enjoyed playing "Rook" and "Parcheesi," and sometimes invited another young Salvation Army couple over from Marysville for dinner and an evening of recreation. To avoid giving offense to their Cornish neighbors, they carefully pulled down the blinds before getting out the game board.

Some American Salvation Army customs were never accepted in Grass Valley. The Sloans had to stand "kettle duty" by themselves at Christmas. The Cornish wanted no part in a form of solicitation that they considered unseemly. Their first Christmas Eve in Grass Valley was a busy one for the young couple. Both had stood kettle duty, and then had supervised the giving out of the Christmas donations of food, clothing and money. When they finally got back home they looked at each other in dismay; neither had bought anything for their own Christmas dinner. But "tes our plaace to take care of the officers," and a basket of food with all the ingredients for a good Christmas dinner was waiting on their doorstep.

The one concession to the new country was in the matter of the lodges. In England, the Salvation Army had tended to oppose its members joining fraternal organizations, perhaps believing that time spent on such affairs showed too much concern with things of this world. When John Hollow, who was Band Sergeant for the Grass Valley unit, became head of the local Oddfellows, Sloan was asked, "Are ye going to stand for that?" But in Grass Valley the Cornish were "joiners," and many of the men belonged to at least one of the local lodges: Oddfellows, Foresters, or Sons of St. George. Opposition would have been fruitless.

Most Cornish were illiterate or only semiliterate, but they had learned the Bible by heart and were able to quote long passages. Sloan remarked that when they came to meetings the miners would appear to be stoic and unemotional, but their feelings ran deep. "Opening up" was hard for them at first, and not all were willing to stand up and give testimony, but when moved by the spirit, emotions would flow and some of the street corner preachers could be impressively fiery.

When called to confess sins, some unusual problems arose. Some miners had "highgraded" and wanted to relieve themselves of both the burden of guilt and the ill-gotten gold, so they would try to hand the nuggets over to the Salvation Army. Sloan was very reluctant to take their offerings, because it was illegal to buy or sell gold without a permit. The culprits would promise never again to take gold from the mine, but the challenge was too much. Even though all miners were expected to walk naked to the showers, and although all lunch buckets were carefully inspected, they would still manage to smuggle out the gold.

Sloan considered the chief fault of the Cornish to be gossip. If someone built an addition to a house or took a trip, the rumors of highgrading would be sure to go the rounds. The private lives of residents of the Methodist Parsonage and the Salvation Army Captain's house were of enduring interest to the gossip mongers, and even the relative amount of garbage in the cans of the leaders of both denominations came in for criticism.

"What about homesickness?" he was asked. "Did the Cornish seem to miss home very much?" Sloan was aware of the tremendous nostalgia for home, but said he felt close to the people and he really believed that they were content in America. Many did go back home, at least for a time. Katie and George Chinn, Louisa George, both Tremewan brothers, and James Bennallack all went home to visit, and a few Cornish stayed permanently, but most found they had developed new roots in California, and most eventually became U.S. citizens.

The Cornish work ethic was certainly one of the major factors responsible for the success of the Cornish in the United States. The English are by no means generally a Puritan people: the work ethic is hardly a tradition in London or the South. In the 17th century the English exported their Puritans, most of whom came from East Anglia. Scotland alone remained Calvinistic, as did the Scots of Northern Ireland. Only with the coming of John Wesley did Puritanism once again become a dominant way of life anywhere south of the Scottish border, and then principally among the industrial working classes of the North and Wales and Cornwall. It is significant that the major proportion of the successful emigration came from the North, East Anglia and Cornwall.

Edward C. Stewart and others have pointed to self-reliance as an American value.[11] The Cornish were by any measure even more self-reliant than the average American. While most Americans accepted such measures as Social Security, and were willing to go to state or local government authorities for help in time of need, the Cornish in our study steadfastly refused aid from outside the family. Mary Kent turned down aid after the death of her husband, preferring to take in boarders. Jane Prior Henwood maintained her independence after she separated from her husband, and even after she became blind she lived alone. Josiah Henwood financed his daughter's college studies, even though the family might reasonably have expected to get some scholarship help.

The men of the second generation preferred to be entrepreneurs rather than work for others. For the women born in America, schoolteaching and business provided the means of independence. Minnie Chinn Farley was "the highest paid girl in Grass Valley" when she married Ed Farley, and she did not marry until she was certain married life was what she wanted.

In the wider American community "getting ahead" is admired. The Cornish appear to have enjoyed taking the initiative; they were capable of making important decisions about their own lives, and preferred activities which challenged their skills and abilities. They also seem, unlike the English but like other Americans, to prefer their achievements to be visible; they are not above a little self-advertisement. This trait has made both Cornish and Americans rather sensitive to praise or blame; the English are not! Competition is part of the "American way of life," and it is also a tradition in Cornish society. The Cornish miner did work as a team member, but usually only with other family members. The team competed with other teams to get the ore out of the ground. This practice may have inhibited labor solidarity, but it heightened family cohesiveness. Significantly, the Cornish sport is wrestling, not a team sport but solely dependent on individual effort.

Stewart has pointed out that American life allows for few deep friendships, and says social life in this country lacks permanence and depth.[12] The Cornish do not seem to follow this social pattern. They seem less anxious to make "acquaintances"; for them friendship is a deep commitment. One is immediately struck by the fact that so many maintained friendships with those they had first known in their home villages. This trait led to criticism that the Cornish were "clannish," and it certainly seems true that, even though the women especially seem to have gone out of their way to help non-Cornish neighbors in trouble, they appear to have formed few friendships outside their own group.

Many non-Cornish Grass Valley residents have warm memories of their Cornish neighbors. Reminiscing about her own childhood, one lady remembered how intrigued she had been by the Cornish houses at Christmas time. Her neighbors decked their houses with holly and mistletoe and, just as in Cornwall, they also strung colored-paper chains from corner to corner in the dining room, and hung paper balls and bells from the center light, imparting a marvelously festive air to family meals.

Another woman remembered how she liked to go to her girl friend's house after school because she would be treated to thick slices of homemade bread spread with butter and "golden syrup." Another person, herself of Irish descent, was more critical of the Cornish. "They never did assimilate," she declared. "They simply took over the town!" But she hastened to add that they were "good people who worked harder than most and deserved what they got."

Of the first generation of Cornish, Rowse estimates 75% were illiterate.[13] However, they valued the opportunities that America provided; they made sure their children would get the education that they had lacked, and when a son or daughter finished high school or a grandchild went off to college, the Cornish family had realized a dream.

Finally, above all else, the Cornish are a proud people, proud of themselves, their families and their Cornish roots. More than one tombstone in a Grass Valley cemetery declares the deceased to be a "Native of Cornwall" rather than of England. The present generation still feels connected to the home county their grandfathers and great-grandfathers left so long ago. The family histories in this book are testimony to an abiding interest in Cornish heritage and the values passed down from the first emigrants.

NOTES

1. "Cornish Wordpower," *Cornish Scene*, Vol 2, No 1, p 4.
2. John Rowe, *The Hardrock Men*, p 1.
3. Edmund Kinyon, "Cornish Migration to Grass Valley," p 3.
4. Bob Paine, "Fool's Gold," *The Union*, March 8, 1969.
5. Susan S. Tamke, *Make a Joyful Noise Unto the Lord*, p 24.
6. E. P. Thompson, *The Making of the English Working Class*, pp 362-374.
7. Gage McKinney, *A High and Holy Place: A Mining Camp Church at New Almaden*, p 20.
8. *Loc. cit.*.
9. A. D. Gilbert, *Religion and Society in Industrial England*, p 87.
10. Bernard Semmel, *Elie Halevy, Methodism and Revolution*, p 19.
11. Edward C. Stewart, *American Culture Patterns*, p 52.
12. *Ibid*, p 54.
13. A. L. Rowse, *The Cousin Jacks*, p 221.

Appendix A

Table I[1]

IMMIGRANTS FROM ENGLAND TO THE UNITED STATES
1820–1950[2]

1821–1830	15,837	1891–1900	216,726
1831–1840	7,611	1901–1910	388,017
1841–1850	32,092	1911–1920	249,944
1851–1860	247,125	1921–1930	157,420
1861–1870	222,277	1931–1940	27,756
1871–1880	431,706	1941–1950	112,252
1881–1890	644,680		

TOTAL 2,753,443

Table II[1]

ENGLISH BORN POPULATION OF THE UNITED STATES
1850–1950

Year	Total Population	Foreign Born	English Born
1850	23,191,876	2,244,602	278,675
1860	31,332,321	4,136,175	431,692
1870	38,558,371	5,567,229	555,046
1880	50,155,783	6,678,943	664,160
1890	62,947,714	9,249,560	909,092
1900	75,994,575	10,341,276	840,513
1910	91,972,266	13,515,886	877,719
1920	105,710,620	13,920,692	813,853
1930	122,775,046	14,204,149	809,563
1940	131,669,275	11,419,138	621,975[3]
1950	150,697,361	10,161,168	554,625[3]

NOTES

1. Derived from the U.S. Bureau of Census Tables (Berthoff 1953:5-7).
2. These figures do not include immigration from Wales, Scotland or Ireland.
3. White English-born only.

Appendix B
Cornish Names and Their History

By Tre, Pol or Pen
Ye may know most Cornishmen
—Ancient Rhyme

Professor A. L. Rowse has suggested that this old saw be rewritten "By Tre, Pol, Car, Ros or Pen . . .," and yet the familiar Celtic prefixes, though still apparent in Cornish names on both sides of the Atlantic, tell only part of the story. There are other names that are just as distinctively Cornish to the person who knows what to look for.

Celtic names, like English names, may be divided into those derived from place names, those derived from occupations, and personal names or nicknames. It seems probable the place names are the most ancient, dating at least as far back as the 400 years during which the Roman Empire extended its domain over most of the British Isles.

The Romans conceived British society as the *plebs* or people; the prefix **Plou-** remains in Breton place names such as Plouville. Society was further divided into *tribus* or families, giving rise to Cornish "tre," Breton "Treve," Welsh "Trif," and Irish "Treabh."[1] Since the tribe and the village came to be synonymous, the term eventually meant "village."

Other place terms reflected as prefixes to Cornish place names include: **Chy-** or **Che-** ("house") as in Chenoweth and Chellew; **Bes-** or **Bos-** ("dwelling") as in Beskeen and Boscawen; **Car-** is "fort" or "earthwork," and **Pen** indicates "the end of," as in Pendelly, which translates as "the end of the copse," and Penhallow, meaning "the end of the marshes." **Pol-** signifies pool, of which there were many kinds in the damp peninsula; thus Polmear is "by the pool," and Polkinghorne is "the pool of Kynkerne," whose name means "Iron Chief."

When surnames were adopted in the middle ages it is not surprising that the old Celtic place names became family names.

Rowse has remarked on the fidelity of these names to the Cornish landscape and its simple peasant way of life:

> ... it is a poor country of hills and slopes, rocks, heaths, marshes, thornbrakes, thickets, withies, broom elders; of cliffs, earthworks, hill forts, long stones, wayside crosses, church enclosures, holly groves, woods and copses broken by patches of cultivation, isolated hamlets, single homesteads by pool or arable, ford or furze bushes. Very little of any urban life appears at all.[2]

Some Celtic names that derive from occupations are still in use, and these include Angove ("the smith"), Tyzak ("the farmer") and Uglow ("the yeoman"). Personal names of Brythonic Celtic origin have most often been translated into English, but a few do remain in their original form. Petherick, Pedrick and Pethick all mean Peter. Vivian or Vyvian is an ancient Celtic name of Cornish origin, and Corin is a beautiful old name whose poetic content Shakespeare recognized.

Many Celtic nicknames survive to the present, including Angwin ("the white or fairheaded man"), and Moyle ("bald"). Teague refers to a "fair" or "beautiful" person, and Hocking means "little fellow." Walls, Walsh, Welch and Welsh denote a "stranger"—any stranger, and not simply one from Wales.

We are familiar with the prefix O' meaning "son of" in Irish names. The O'Briens, O'Shaugnessys and O'Sullivans are easily recognized as sons of Erin. Fewer realize that the Cornish use the "O" as a suffix; thus Jago ("son of James"), Kitto ("son of Kitt"), and Benneto ("son of Bennet") are Cornish names. One must be careful in this category, however, for not all such endings mean "son of." Bosanko, for example, was probably once Bosanketh, meaning "dwelling in the woods," and Spargo, a common name among the Cornish in the U.S., means simply "thornbrake," a place name. John Spargo (1876–1966), a pioneer labor leader, wrote an excellent family history in which he traced this name back to the hamlets of Upper Spargo and Lower Spargo in the Parish of Mabe near Falmouth.[3]

The Cornish language ceased to be spoken by the end of the 18th century, but long before that, English first and last names had been adopted by the large majority of the Cornish people, and today English names predominate. Richard Blewett's analysis of names from the 1953 list of voters in Cornwall found only ten percent of names to be of Celtic derivation, while the rest were names common to the rest of England.[4] This is no less true in the U.S., where most Cornish have English last names, and it is therefore necessary to check family records and traditions before one can presume that any particular family is of Cornish ancestry.

For obvious reasons, few Cornish families bear surnames derived from English place names, but English occupational names such as Taylor, Cooper, Smith and Sawyer are quite common. Of the large class of last names derived from personal names, some are rather more likely to be Cornish: Harry, Tom, George, Paul and John are of this class, and any of these may carry the suffix -s (or less frequently, -son) to indicate "son of." The Cornish seem to have had a particular penchant for Biblical names, and last names such as Boaz, Abraham(s), Jacob(s) and Job(e) are quite likely to be Cornish.

Nicknames used as last names have some peculiar Cornish quirks: Knee and Kneebone, Foot(e), Ankle, Neck and Chinn are not uncommon, either in Cornwall or among the Cousin Jacks, but one would have to inquire as to family and ethnic background; Chinn, for instance, could quite as well be Chinese.

In the Grass Valley census of 1870, out of a total of 7,251 people, 140 Cornish names can be found, with an additional large number of English names that might very well be Cornish. Since many names are duplicated, the total number of people represented is well over 1,000.

The 1978 Pacific Bell Telephone Directory listed a total of some 1,435 families in the Grass Valley/Nevada City section, and of these no fewer than 155 had old Cornish names of Celtic origin, while at least 850 more had names that were English but might belong to Cornish families and are of the "occupation," "nickname" and "personal name" classes.

COMMON CORNISH SURNAMES

Abraham or Abrahams; Adams; Allen; Andrew or Andrews; Andrewartha; Andrews; Angove ("blacksmith"); Angrave; Angwin ("white or fairheaded man"); Ankle; Argall ("retreat" or "shelter"); Arthur; Axford.

Bailey; Barkel; Barling; Barmes; Barmett; Barrett; Barron; Bartle; Basset; Bastian; Batten; Bawden; Benalleck or Benallick or Bennallack ("broomrake"); Benbow; Bennet or Bennets or Bennett or Bennetts; Benneto ("son of Bennet"); Berriman or Berryman; Berry; Bettalack; Bettis; Bice; Bickford; Billings; Bishop; Blackwell; Blewett or Bluett; Blight; Boase or Boaz ("dwelling"); Bolitho; Bone; Bosanketh and Bosanko ("dwelling in the wood"); Bosustow; Bottrell; Bowden; Bray ("hill"); Brent; Brokenshire; Buckley; Buddle; Bullock; Bunney; Burden; Burgan; Burge; Buzza.

Caddy; Cann; Carbis; Cargile; Carkeek; Carlis; Carlyon; Carne; Carskadon; Carter; Certhew; Chalmers; Champion; Chapman; Chegwidden; Chellew or Chellow ("house by pool" or "house of Lew"); Chenoweth or Chynoweth ("new house"); Chew; Chinn; Chirgwin; Christoe; ("new house"); Clemo or Clemow or Climo or Clyma or Clymo ("dweller on slopes" or "son of Clem"); Cliff; Coad; Cock; Cocking; Colenso; Collick; Collins; Colliver; Combellack; Connibear; Cook; Cooley; Coomb or Coombe or Coombes ("little valley"); Coon or Coons ("dog man"); Copeland; Cord; Corin (old first name); Cornish ("Cornishman"); Couch ("redhaired" or "redfaced"); Coulson; Cowling; Cox; Crace or Crays or Craze or Crase ("middle" of a place); Crapp; Cudlip; Cundy ("house of the dog man"); Curnow ("Cornishman").

Dale; Daley; Daniell; Darke; Davey or Davy; Deeble or Dibble; Dennis; Dingle; Doidge; Drew; Dunstan or Dunstone; Dyer.

Easterbrook; Eddy; Ede; Edgcomb; Edwards; Ellery; Ennis ("island" or "peninsula"); Ennor ("the boundary"); Esterbrook; Euda; Eudy; Eva (old first name); Evans.

Faull; Fenton ("spring" or "well"); Ferrel; Fitzsimmons; Floyd; Foot or Foote; Foxwell; Francis; Furze.

Gale; Gartrell; Geach; George; Gidley; Gilbert; Gillis; Glassen or Glasson; Glendenning; Gluyas; Godfrey; Goldsworth or Goldsworthy ("field of the fair" or "feast"); Green; Gregor; Grenfel or Grenfall or Grenfell; Grey; Gribble; Grigg; Gundry.

Hall; Hancock; Harper; Harris; Harry; Hart; Hawe; Hawken; Haws; Hay; Heather; Hender; Hendra; Henwood ("old wood"); Hendy; Hichens; Hicks; Hitchens; Hoar or Hoare; Hocking ("little fellow"); Hodge; Hodges; Hollow; Holman; Hooper; Hosken or Hoskin or Hosking or Hoskins ("sedge marsh"); Hugh; Humphrey; Hunkin.

Inch; Ingram; Isaac; Ivey or Ivie or Ivy.

Jack; Jacka; Jago or Jagoe ("son of James"); Jacob or Jacobs; James; Jenkin or Jenkins; Jennings; Jewel or Jewell (from "St. Juhel" or "St Judicael"); Job or Jobe; John or Johns; Jollif; Jose; Juleff.

Keast; Kent ("people of the corner"); Kessel or Kissell or Kistle; King; Kingdon; Kinsman; Kinyon, Kitt; Kitto or Kittoe ("son of Kitt"); Knapp; Knee; Kneebone; Knight; Kornish ("Cornishman").

Laity; Lander ("churchyard" or "enclosure"); Langdon; Lanyon ("bleak enclosure" or "pool"); Lawrey; Leah ("flat stone"); Leahy ("flat stone"); Lean ("stitch of land" or "pool"); Legg; Levering; Lewarne; Liddicoat or Lidicote; Lobb; Lory; Lugg; Luke.

Mantle; Martin; Masters; Mathew or Matthews; Maynard; Mello or Mellow; Menet or Menhennet or Menhennick ("parish of the long stone" [menhir]); Merrifield; Mewten; Mill; Millet; Minear or Miner or Miners ("stone" [menhir]); Mitchel or Mitchell; Morcam; Morrish; Moyle ("bald"); Murton.

Nance ("valley"); Nancollis; Nankervis ("valley of the deer"); Neal; Neck; Nettel or Nettle; Nicholas or Nichols; Ninnis; Noall or Noell; Northey; Nye.

Oates; Oatey; Odgers; Olds; Opie or Oppy; Osbiston; Osborne; Owsley.

Painter or Paynter; Parkin or Parkyn; Parnell; Parsons; Pasco or Pascoe ("Easter child"); Paul or Paull; Pearce or Pierce; Pedinnin; Pell or Pells; Pellar or Peller; Pello or Pellow or

Pellowe or Pillow ("roundheaded"); Penaluna or Peneluna ("end of grove or pool"); Penberthy; Pengelley or Pengilley ("end of the copse"); Penglace or Penglase; Penhallow; Penna ("hilltop" or "summit"); Pennell or Penole; Penpraze; Penrose ("top of the heath"); Perrin; Peters; Phillip or Phillips; Polglaise or Polglase or Polglaze ("green pool"); Polhemus; Polkinghorne; Pollard; Polmear; Pomeroy; Pope; Prater; Prideaux; Prisk; Prouse or Prowse; Prout; Pryor.

Quick; Ralph; Rapson; Rawlins; Reese; Renowden; Reseigh; Retallack or Retallic or Retallick ("steep hill spur"); Reynolds; Richards or Rickard; Roach; Robert or Roberts; Robins or Robbins; Rodda (old first name); Rodgers or Rogers; Roe or Rowe; Rolfe; Rosevear or Rosevere or Rosewear ("big heath" or "moor"); Rosewarren; Roskilley; Rouse or Rowse; Royce; Rule ("furrow" or "cleft"); Rumphery; Rundle.

Sampson; Scadden or Scaddon; Scobel or Scoble or Scovell; Searle; Semmen or Semens or Simmonds or Simmons or Symons; Shephard; Shin or Shinn; Shugg; ; Sims; Sincock; Sinnott; Skewers; Skewes or Skewis or Skews ("sheltered place"); Sleeman; Smith; Snell; Sobey; Southey; Spargo ("thorn brake"); Stacey; Stanway; Stenlake; Stephens or Stevens; Stocks; Stoddart; Stratton; Strike; Strongman.

Talleck; Tallon; Tamblyn; Tangye; Teague ("fair" or "beautiful"); Tenberth; Terrell or Terrill or Turrell or Tyrrell; Thomas; Tierney; Tink; Tippett; Thomas; Tonkin; Tom or Toms; Toy; Trathan or Trathen ("sandy place"); Trebilcock or Trebilcocks or Trebilcox or Triblecox; Trebotich; Tredinick or Tredinnick; Tredrea; Treganowan ("homestead at mouth or hollow"); Tregarning; Tregaskis ("homestead in sheltered place"); Tregloan; Tregonning; Trelawn; Treloar or Trelore ("homestead with garden"); Tremain or Tremaine ("homestead by the stone"); Trembarth or Trembath or Tremberth or Tremberthy; Tremellen or Tremelling; Tremewan ("homestead of Ewan]"); Tremoureux; Trenberth; Trenear; Trengove; Trengrove; Trenmell; Trennary; Trerew; Trescott or Truscott; Tresidder; Tresize or Trezise; Trestrail; Trethewey; Trevenna ("homestead on the hill"); Trevethick or Trevidick or

Trevithick; Trevillion or Trevillyan or Trevithan; Trevorrow; Trewarkus; Trewartha; Treweek; Trewella or Trewhella ("homestead by the stream"); Trewen or Trewyn; Treworjy; Trezona; Triplett; Truan; ("across the wood"); Tucker; Tyacke, Tyzak ("farmer").

Uglow ("yeoman"); Uren ("swamp" or "marsh"); Varcoe; Veal or Vial ("Mael"—a personal name); Venning; Vine; Vivian or Vyvyan.

Wakefield; Wales or Wallace or Wallis or Walsh or Welch or Welsh ("stranger"); Warne or Wearne or Warren ("swamp"); Waters; Wear; Webb; Wedge; Werry; Whale; White; Whittle; Wicks; Wilcox; Willey; Williams; Willoughby; Wilton; Winn; Woolcock; Worth; Wyatt.

NOTES

1. John Morris, *The Age of Arthur*, p 459.
2. A. L. Rowse, *The Cousin Jacks*, p 428.
3. John Spargo, *Notes on the Name and Family of Spargo*, p 9.
4. Rowse, *The Cousin Jacks*, p 427.

Appendix C
Mining Terms

Adit Drainage Tunnel. Strictly speaking, any more or less horizontal passage into the mine.

Attle Waste or "dead" rock.

Bal (*Cornish*) Mine.

Bal Maiden Woman who worked at mine. In 19th century Cornwall, women "dressed" the ore, breaking the rock down to the proper size for easy separation of the metallic content. Eventually, the introduction of stamping machines eliminated this function (see **Spalling**).

Black Powder Gunpowder, introduced for blasting in 1670.

Boryer (*Cornish*) Drill rod for boring holes. Two techniques were used. In "single jacking" one miner held both boryer and a three-pound hammer. In "double jacking" the miner worked with a partner, one wielding an eight-pound hammer with both hands while the partner twisted the boryer. Except for men from the St. Just area, Cornish miners preferred "double jacking," and their opposition to the practice of the one-handed technique was a contributory cause of the 1869 strike in Grass Valley.

Buddle (*Cornish*) Flat sloping trough used to process ore. In 19th-century Cornwall, buddling was performed by small boys. The buddle was filled with ore and set in a stream. The boys trod the ore to pulverize it and speed the separation of metal from waste.

Bucca (*Cornish*) One of the "Little People" said to live in the mines (see **Knocker**).

Captain Mine supervisor. Captains were drawn from the ranks of working miners.

Core (*Cornish*) Shift.

Cornish Pumping Engine Accumulated water in the mines was a problem from earliest times. In 1801 the Cornish Pumping Engine was invented and was subsequently used widely, both in Cornwall and in America. The machine consisted of a rod, constructed in sections and possibly as long as 3,000 feet, pushed by a "walking beam" and attached to the pumping engine. The rod simultaneously operated a series of pumps. Each pump delivered its load of water into a tank from which the next higher pump drew its supply, and so on to the surface.[1]

Croust (*Cornish*) Snack or lunch.

Galleries Regular compartments dividing the lode. Each gallery was about 300 feet long and 60 feet high. Galleries were subdivided by small perpendicular shafts into "pitches" (see **Pitch**).[2]

Giant Powder Dynamite was first introduced on the Pacific Coast under the name of Giant Powder in 1867. . . . The mining superintendents in the Grass Valley district began experimenting with it in the latter part of 1868. Although at $1.25 a pound giant powder was much more expensive than black powder at 11 cents a pound, some mining superintendents found it could reduce the cost of ore extraction. . . . Where two men were needed to drill the large holes required for a charge of black powder, a single man could drill the smaller holes that sufficed for the more powerful giant powder. This change from double- to single-handed drilling reduced the mining crews by nearly half, more than offsetting the higher cost of the powder." For this reason, also because of the ill-effects of the noxious gasses produced, the Cornish opposed the use of dynamite for several years.[3]

Gig Platform type elevator cage used for hauling small numbers of men to and from the surface.

Grass Surface of mine head. ("To grass"—at the surface.)

Highgrading Stealing ore from the mine. Legally, to break a piece of gold-bearing quartz and bring it up from the mine was not theft, just trespass. Only after the rock had been broken down was its removal theft.[4]

Hydraulicking Hydraulic mining was the blasting of a hillside with a high-pressure stream of water delivered through a large "gune" or nozzle. With a hydraulic pipe, one or two men could process hundreds of tons of earth daily. Nevada County's Malakoff Diggings (at North Bloomfield) was the world's largest hydraulic mining operation. Downstream farmers became increasingly concerned over the silting-up of the Yuba, Feather and Sacramento Rivers, and in 1884 restrictions against dumping tailings into rivers and streams ended hydraulicking.

Jigging Washing ore to rid it of its impurities. In Cornwall this was done by children (see **Buddle**).

Kibble (*Cornish*) Bucket used for hauling up ore.

Knacked (*Cornish*) Dead. ("A knack'd bal"—a dead or abandoned mine.)

Knockers Little People thought to live and work in the mines. Although they were said to look after the miners by warning them of impending disaster, they were also supposed to be full of mischief, blowing out candles, hiding tools, and showering down small stones. (Also known as **Tommyknockers** in California.)[5]

Leat (*Cornish*) Stream.

Lode Vein or strata of ore-bearing rock. The lode was divided into regular compartments known as "galleries" (see **Galleries**).

Mother Lode Coloma, El Dorado County [California], site of James Marshall's discovery of gold on January 24, 1848, early was regarded as the approximate dividing point between southern and northern gold fields. Later, quartz miners found a system of ore veins they called the Mother Lode running rope-like up through the Southern Mines and ending near Georgetown, close to Coloma.[6]

Northern Mines A distinct entity, separate from the Mother Lode and centered around Grass Valley and Nevada City, and extending throughout Nevada, Sierra, Yuba, Butte and Plumas counties.

Pare (*Cornish*) Work group of miners. Two or three men and one or two boys, often all members of the same family.

Placer Mining (*Spanish*) Small-scale placer mining is simply digging in sand and gravel deposits with pick and shovel. Large-scale operations involve power shovels, bucket-wheel excavators, or dragline conveyors which deliver the gravel to a system of screens, jigs and sluices in order to recover the mineral (see **Streaming**).

Pitch Small perpendicular shafts divided each gallery into pitches about 60 feet high and 30 feet long. In Cornwall, miners bid competitively in order to work a pitch.[7]

Skip A sloping elevator car with seats, used to haul large numbers of men in and out of the mine. The skip was powered by a "steam whim."

Spalling Pounding ore with a hammer, a first step in the extraction of the metal. In 19th-century Cornwall, spalling was work for the "bal maidens."

Stamp Mill Spalling the ore was soon abandoned when stamp mills came into use. The earliest mill on Wolf Creek in Grass Valley had iron-capped logs as stamps and was steam- powered. Later, iron stamps in sets of five came into service; these were eventually powered by electricity.

Stoping The technique of excavating the ore; the stope is the working surface of the lode.

Streaming The Cornish version of placer mining. Large wooden bowls had been used in Cornwall to pan for particles of tin long before the California gold rush.

Stull Massive timber support for the mine roof.

Tommyknockers (see **Knockers**)

Tributers "Pares" or teams of men who functioned as independent contractors. Tributer groups bid against each other for the pitch they would work, and then were paid a proportion of the value of the ore won. According to Lingenfelter, tributing, the most popular system among Cornish miners in England was employed very selectively and generally to the disadvantage of the miner in America and for this reason was opposed by miners unions.[8]

Tutworkers (*Cornish/English*) Taskworkers who provided their own tools, candles and dynamite and were paid a set amount per unit of work done, e.g., per fathom advanced, square fathom of lode stoped, or weight of deposit mined. This system was not used in the U.S., where the contract was for labor only, and the company provided the candles, tools, etc.

Vug (*Cornish*) Hollow space.

Wheal (*Cornish*) Mine. According to Dexter, "wheal" names are not as old as "bal" names in the designations of mines. Some mines are named after Cornish families: Wheal Basset, Wheal Vyvian. Some are female names: Wheal Frances, Wheal Kitty. Some are sentimental names: Wheal Fortune, Wheal Hope. A few show Puritan influence: Wheal Romoth, Wheal Zion. Rather few are real Cornish names: Wheal Coates ("coid"—wood), Wheal Penrose ("Penrose"—end of heath).[9]

Whim   (*Cornish*) Engine.

Winze (Whinze)   (*Cornish*) Small internal mine shaft.

Winze Brace   (*Cornish/English*) Windlass and tackle.

NOTES

1. Jim Morley and Doris Foley, *Gold Cities*, p 45.
2. Cecil Todd, *The Cornish Miner in America*, p 23.
3. Richard E. Lingenfelter, *The Hardrock Miners*, p 83.
4. *Ibid*, p 82.
5. John Vivian, *Tales of the Cornish Miners*, p 12; Elmer E. Stevens, "The Cornish Miner," p 3.
6. Morley and Foley, p 4.
7. Todd, p 23.
8. Lingenfelter, p 20.
9. T. F. G. Dexter, *Cornish Names*, p 48.

Appendix D
Cornish Food

In 19th-century rural Cornwall, cooking was done either over the open fire or in a "cloam oven." This was an oval or oblong earthenware oven built into the side wall of the fireplace chimney. To heat it, the housewife set sticks or bundles of furze inside and set fire to them. When the ashes were white they were raked out and the oven was ready. The food was put inside, a clay door set in place, and the food baked with the heat from the fireplace. Pasties, saffron buns and "splits" (scones) all came out of the cloam oven, and the larger ones might even hold a Christmas goose.*

Cornish food was hearty, as it had to be to support people doing hard physical work. Potatoes were a staple as ingredients in soups and stews and in the famous Cornish pasties, where they were combined with other vegetables (usually onions and turnips) and such beef as the housewife could afford. It might well be noted, however, that Cornish women were famous for putting into pasties almost anything they had handy, so rabbit, and also various seasonal vegetables such as broccoli, might easily end up in a pasty. 'Tis said the reason the devil never crossed the Tamar into Cornwall was for fear of being popped into a pasty!

---

* Mary Wright, *Cornish Treats*, p 4.

Sibley Bennallack Hansen, Ardith Phelan and others making pasties in the Grass Valley Methodist Church in 1998.

Recipes*

CORNISH PASTIES Pasties are always eaten from the hand. Start at the end without the initial. If the pasty has to be laid down, the owner will recognize it! (Makes 2)

Pastry: 1½ cups flour
3/4 teaspoons salt
½ cup shortening
3 Tablespoons water

Filling: ½ pound good chuck steak
2 or 3 potatoes
1 onion
1 turnip (if liked)
salt and pepper

1. **Pastry:** Mix flour and salt. Rub in fat (use your fingers, mix will look like cornmeal). Add water, drop by drop, stirring with fork, then work with hands into 2 balls. Rest in cool place. Then roll out into 8" rounds ¼" thick. (*Note: This pastry uses less fat than typical U.S. recipes. Pastry should be "firm."*)

2. **Filling:** Cut meat into small pieces. Slice potato (and turnip, if liked) thinly. Finely chop onion.

3. Take pastry round. Starting ½" from edge, put layer of potatoes to cover half pastry. Then turnips. Then meat, and finally onions. Do not cover more than half pastry. Add salt and pepper to taste.

4. Dampen edges of top (unfilled) half.

5. Bring unfilled side over to filled side. Press two sides together and crimp with thumb and finger.

6. Put a slit in top and mark the initials of the owner at one end.

7. Cook in pre-heated oven. 400 degrees F for 30 minutes, then 350 degrees for next 30 minutes.

---

* All of these recipes are from the collection of my grandmother, Charlotte (Lottie) E. Turner, who for many years was manager of the Pedn-Olva Hotel, St. Ives, Cornwall.

SAFFRON BUNS were typically given to children at Cornish "Tea Treats" or Sunday School picnics.

> 1 package active dry yeast
> 1/4 cup warm water
> 1 cup milk
> 1/4 cup sugar
> 1 teaspoonful salt
> 1/4 cup shortening
> 4 cups flour
> 3/4 cups currants
>   (or 1/2 cup currants, 1/4 cup peel)
> 1/8 teaspoonful saffron

1. Scald milk
   Add: All but 1/2 teaspoon sugar
      Shortening
      Salt
      Saffron
   Cool mixture to luke warm.

2. Put 1/2 teaspoon sugar in luke warm water
   Add yeast
   Stir and leave for 5 minutes.

3. Add yeast mixture to milk mixture.

4. Add 1 1/2 cups of flour. Beat vigorously 1 minute.
   Cover. Let rise in warm place until very light.

5. Add rest of flour and fruit, kneading until bowl is clean and you have a smooth ball of dough.

6. Put in greased bowl. Grease top of dough. Cover with clean towel. Let rise until doubled.

7. Make 24 smooth little balls.
   Set on greased cooked sheets.
   Cover and let stand about 15 minutes.

8. Bake 15–20 minutes at 375 degrees F.

CORNISH BUCKET CAKES were made by the miners' wives to provide a treat in the lunch buckets. These buckets had two sections. Hot tea went in the bottom, the pasty next and then bucket cakes or other sweet cakes on top.

When Ed and Minnie Chinn Farley were interviewed (see Chapters 7 and 11), Minnie was making Cornish Cream. The big shallow granite crock was standing on the counter in the sunny kitchen. She had slowly cooked the cream, and it was setting and ready to be skimmed. That evening's supper consisted of a thick pink slice of ham, and potato salad, followed by the thick cream on a strawberry jam tart. Minnie also served Bucket Cakes.

3 cups flour
¾ teaspoon salt
1 cup sugar
1½ teaspoonsful baking powder
½ teaspoonful soda
1 cup shortening (margarine)
2 eggs, beaten
6 Tablespoons milk
1 cup currants

1. Sift dry ingredients.

2. Blend in margarine (use fingers).

3. Add milk, eggs, currants.

4. Pat out to ½" thickness. Cut with cookie cutter (Grandma used a small cup) into 1½" circles.

5. Cook over low heat on greased griddle or frying pan.

Bibliography

BARTON, R. M., *Life in Cornwall in the Early Nineteenth Century: Being Extracts from the West Briton Newspaper in the Quarter Century from 1810 to 1835.* Truro: D. Bradford Barton, 1970.

———. *Life in Cornwall in the Mid Nineteenth Century: Being Extracts from the West Briton Newspaper in the Two Decades from 1835 to 1854.* Truro: D. Bradford Barton, 1971.

———. *Life in Cornwall in the Late Nineteenth Century: Being Extracts from the West Briton Newspaper in the Two Decades from 1855 to 1875.* Truro: D. Bradford Barton, 1972.

———. *Life in Cornwall at the End of the Nineteenth Century: Being Extracts from the West Briton Newspaper in the Years from 1876 to 1899.* Truro: D. Bradford Barton, 1973.

BERRY, CLAUDE. *Cornwall.* London: Robert Hale, 1949.

BERTHOFF, ROWLAND TAPPAN. *British Immigrants in Industrial America 1792–1950.* Cambridge: Harvard University Press, 1953.

BRAMMELL, KATHLEEN LESLIE. *Cornish Miners of Grass Valley and Nevada County.* Unpublished M.A. Thesis. Chico, CA: Chico State University, 1972.

BRITISH PARLIAMENTARY PAPERS. *Children's Employment Commission. First Report of the Commissioners, Mines. Industrial Revolution, Children's Employment, Vol 6 1846.* Shannon: Irish University Press, 1968.

BURKE, GILL. "The Decline of the Independent Bal Maiden: The Impact of Change in the Cornish Mining Industry," *Unequal Opportunities: Women's Employment in England 1800–1918,* edited by Angela V. John. Oxford: Basil Blackwell, 1986.

CARROTHERS, W. A. *Emigration from the British Isles.* London: P. S. King, 1929. (Reprinted New York: Augustus M. Kelley, 1969.)

COOK, JUDITH. *Close to the Earth: Living Social History of the British Isles.* London: Routledge & Kegan Paul, 1984.

DEXTER, T. F. G. *Cornish Names.* London: Longmans, Green and Co., 1926. (Reprinted Truro: D. Bradford Barton, 1968.)

DU MAURIER, DAPHNE. *Vanishing Cornwall.* New York: Doubleday, 1967.

EARL, BRYAN. *Cornish Mining: The Techniques of Metal Mining in the West of England, Past and Present*. Truro: D. Bradford Barton, 1968.

ERICKSON, CHARLOTTE. *Invisible Immigrants: The Adaptation of English and Scottish Emigrants in Nineteenth Century America*. London: London School of Economics and Political Science, 1972.

EWART, SHIRLEY. "Names: Their Meaning and Occurrence in Nevada County," *Nevada County Historical Society Bulletin*, Vol 34, No 2, April 1980.

————. "Cornish Miners in Grass Valley: The Letters of John Coad, 1858–1860," *The Pacific Historian*, Vol 25, No 4, Winter 1981.

————. *Cornish Mining Families in Grass Valley, California*. New York: AMS Press, 1989.

————. "Cornish," *Encyclopedia of American Immigrant Cultures*. New York: Macmillan, 1997.

FOLEY, DORIS E. "A Breath of Old Cornwall," *Nevada County Historical Society Bulletin*, Vol 7, No 4, December 1953.

————. "Another First for Nevada County, Part II," *Nevada County Historical Society Bulletin*, Vol 3, No 6, October 1950.

GEORGE, HAROLD J. "Grass Valley Cornish Carol Choir," *Nevada County Historical Society Bulletin*, Vol 7, No 4, December 1953.

GILBERT, A. D. *Religion and Society in Industrial England*. London: Longman, 1976.

GUINN, CINDY. *Harold Jewell George*. Unpublished Paper, 1978.

HARRIES, NORMAN H. *Cornish and Welsh Mining Settlements in California*. Unpublished M.A. Thesis. Berkeley: University of California, 1956.

JENKIN, A. K. HAMILTON. *The Cornish Miner*. London: George Allen and Unwin, 1927.

————. *Cornwall and Its People*. London: J. M. Dent and Sons, 1945.

KEMBLE, JOHN HASKELL. *The Panama Route 1848–1869*. Berkeley: University of California Press, 1945.

KINYON, EDMUND. "Cornish Migration to Grass Valley," *Nevada County Historical Society Bulletin*. Vol 3, No 6, October 1950.

LEIFCHILD, J. R. *Cornwall and Its Mines and Miners*. London: Longman, Brown, Green and Robert, 1857. (Reprinted New York: Augustus M. Kelley, 1969.)

LINGENFELTER, RICHARD E. *The Hardrock Miners: A History of the Mining Labor Movement in the American West 1863–1893*. Berkeley: University of California Press, 1974.

MANN, RALPH. "The Decade After the Gold Rush: Social Structure in Grass Valley and Nevada City, California 1850–1860," *Pacific Historical Review*, Vol XLI, No 4, November 1972.

————. *After the Gold Rush: Society in Grass Valley and Nevada City, California 1849–1870*. Stanford: Stanford University Press, 1982.

MCKINNEY, GAGE. *A High and Holy Place: A Mining Camp Church at New Almaden*. New Almaden, CA: New Almaden County Quicksilver Park Association, 1997.

MICHELL, FRANK. *Annals of an Ancient Cornish Town: Redruth*. Redruth: Dyllansow Truran, 1978.

MINTER, JOHN EASTER. *The Chagres: River of Westward Passage*. New York: Rinehart, 1948.

MORLEY, JIM AND DORIS FOLEY. *Gold Cities: Grass Valley and Nevada City*. Berkeley: Howell-North, 1965.

MORRIS, JOHN. *The Age of Arthur*. New York: Charles Scribner's Sons, 1973.

PAINE, ROBERT. "Fools Gold," *The Union*, Grass Valley, CA, March 8, 1969.

RICKARD, T. A. *A History of American Mining*. New York: McGraw Hill, 1932.

ROWE, JOHN. *Cornwall in the Age of the Industrial Revolution*. Liverpool: Liverpool University Press, 1953.

————. *The Hardrock Men: Cornish Immigrants and the North American Mining Frontier*. London: Barnes and Noble, 1974.

ROWE, LAURA M. GRIBBEN. "Cornish Wrestling in Nevada County." *Nevada County Historical Society Bulletin*. Vol 23, No 4, July 1969.

ROWSE, A. L. *The Cousin Jacks: The Cornish in America*. New York: Charles Scribner's Sons, 1969.

SAMUEL, RAPHAEL (ED). "Mineral Workers," *Miners, Quarrymen and Saltworkers*. London: Routledge & Kegan Paul, 1977.

SEMMEL, BERNARD. *Elie Halevy, Methodism and Revolution*. Chicago: University of Chicago Press, 1971.

SHEPPERSON, WILLIAM S. *British Immigrants to North America*. Minneapolis: University of Minnesota Press, 1957.

SPARGO, JOHN. *Notes on the Name and Family of Spargo*. Old Bennington, VT: John Spargo, 1945.

STEVENS, ELMER E. "The Cornish Miner," *Nevada County Historical Society Bulletin*, Vol 18, No 1, March 1964.

STEWART, EDWARD C. *American Culture Patterns: A Cross Cultural Perspective*. Washington, D.C.: Society for Intercultural Education, Training and Research, 1972.

TAMKE, SUSAN S. *Make a Joyful Noise Unto the Lord: Hymns as a Reflection of Victorian Social Attitudes*. Athens: Ohio University Press, 1978.

TAYLOR, PHILIP. *The Distant Magnet: European Emigration to the U.S.A.*. London: Eyre and Spottiswoode, 1971.

THOMPSON, E. P. *The Making of the English Working Class*. New York: Vintage Books, 1966.

TODD, ARTHUR CECIL. *The Cornish Miner in America*. Glendale, CA: The Arthur H. Clark Co., 1967. (Reprinted Spokane: The Arthur H. Clark Co., 1995.)

TRAILL, CATHERINE PARR. *The Canadian Settler's Guide*. Toronto: The Old Countryman's Office, 1855. (Reprinted Toronto: McClelland and Stewart, 1969.)

VIVIAN, JOHN. *Tales of the Cornish Miners*. Truro: Tor Mark Press, 1960.

WELLS, HARRY L., J. ALBERT WILSON, H. B. RICE, AND ALLEN M. FREEMAN. *History of Nevada County, California*. Oakland: Thompson and West, 1880. (Reprinted Berkeley: Howell-North, 1970.)

WRIGHT, MARY. *Cornish Treats*. Penzance: Alison Hodge, 1986.

NEWSPAPERS

California Daily Courier, San Francisco.
Golden Era, San Francisco.
Grass Valley National, Grass Valley.
Grass Valley Telegraph, Grass Valley.
Grass Valley Union, Grass Valley.
Nevada National, Grass Valley.
Nevada Transcript, Nevada City.

JOURNALS

Cornish Scene. Highshore House, New Bridge St., Truro TR1 2AA.

Cornish World: The International Magazine for the Cornish. Cornish World Publications, The Institute of Cornish Studies, Trevithick Centre, Trevenson Rd. Redruth, Cornwall TR15 3PL.

Tam Kernewek. The Cornish American Heritage Society. Editor N. Heydt, 5 Hampton Court, Neptune, NJ 07753-5672.

Index

NEVADA COUNTY PIONEERS SERIES

Nevada County Vital Statistics 1850–1869
by David A. and Ardis H. Comstock

Highly Respectable Families: The Cornish of
Grass Valley, California 1854–1954
by Shirley Ewart with Harold T. George